AFRICA
THE WAY AHEAD

AFRICA
THE WAY AHEAD

by

Jack Woddis

INTERNATIONAL PUBLISHERS
NEW YORK

Printed in the United States of America

To my daughters,
JANE AND JOANNA,
who will live to see a
glorious new Africa

"Who is the enemy?
The enemy is imperialism, which uses as its weapons colonialism and neo-colonialism."
> (President Kwame Nkrumah, in his speech to the Conference of African Freedom Fighters, Accra, 4 June 1962.)

INTRODUCTION TO AMERICAN EDITION

Within a few months of my writing the Introduction to the English edition of *Africa, The Way Ahead*, an event of historic importance took place in Africa, further confirming that the tide of African revolution is still flowing fast and is rising ever higher. This event was the holding of the Conference of Independent African States at Addis Ababa on May 22 to 25, 1963, resulting in an agreement to establish the Organisation of African Unity, the adoption of a Charter of African Unity as the instrument for this organisation, and the taking of decisions to hasten the liberation of all African territories still under foreign domination.

This was the third conference of independent African states. The first was held at Accra, April 15-22, 1958. It was attended by all eight independent African states which existed at that time. At the second conference, held at Addis Ababa, June 15-24, 1960, there were 12 African states represented. The historic third conference, also held at Addis Ababa, was attended by the heads of 30 independent African states, and the remaining two states, Morocco and Togo, were also represented, though not by their heads of state. These 32 independent African states represented 212 million African people. In addition, there were present at the conference a number of delegates from 21 national parties representing those African states still under colonial rule, and in which live some 40 million African people.

Indicative of the quick changes taking place in Africa is the fact that, at the time of writing, Kenya and Zanzibar have now won their political independence and will be celebrating this achievement in December 1963, and Malawi (Nyasaland) will be doing the same in July 1964. It is confidently expected that Zambia (Northern Rhodesia) will follow suit a few months later.

* * *

The first two conferences of independent African states had taken important decisions which helped to pave the way for further advance. But imperialist intrigues over the past two years, the neo-colonialist activities of American imperialism, and the actions of British and French imperialists, as well as their rivalry one with the other, combined to bring about what appeared to be serious divisions between the African states and their leaders and led to the formation of different groupings of African states, one known as the Casablanca group and regarded as the more progressive, and the other called the Brazzaville group, later the Monrovia group, and generally regarded as more conservative. Within this latter group there is also the separate Union of African and Malagasy States, closely tied to French imperialism.

On the eve of the Addis Ababa conference, the Western press was full of prophecies of difficulties and divisions. Even as late as May 23, after the conference had already opened, the London *Times* commented that the character of the practical arrangements "bodes ill for any attempts to get unity organised on a competent basis."

These gloomy prognostications in the Western press were not simply the outcome of their lack of appreciation of the strength and breadth of the African revolution; rather, they were an expression of the tactics of the imperialists who were concerned to play up the differences among the African leaders in the hope of spreading distrust and despondency and so maintain the divisions.

But all these hopes came to nothing. The conference resulted in an historic advance for the African people and a resounding rebuff to the imperialists. The watchword of the conference became unity. All decisions received the unanimous support of the delegates—and the decisions were of a character that themselves help forward the cause of African unity.

Unity without a clear policy or direction would have been of limited value. But the whole significance of the unity achieved at the Addis Ababa conference was that it was *a unity directed against imperialism, colonialism, and neo-colonialism, and in favour of peace.*

On the very eve of the conference, the influential Ghana weekly journal, *The Spark* (May 17, 1963), carried a front page article significantly entitled "Anti-Imperialist United Africa is the Goal".

The Addis Ababa Conference took two major decisions which carry forward this anti-imperialist aim.

The first was the establishment of a permanent organ of the independent states of Africa in the form of the Organisation of African Unity, and the adoption of a Charter for its functioning.

The second was the setting up of a special Coordinating Committee or National Liberation Bureau, which will be responsible for coordinating the efforts of the independent states in their activities to "accelerate the unconditional attainment of national independence by all African territories still under foreign domination."

These measures include concerted efforts by the independent states in the United Nations and other international bodies; the breaking off of diplomatic relations with Portugal and South Africa; economic sanctions against these reactionary powers; help to unite the national liberation movements in the different colonial territories still remaining; and the setting up of a Co-ordinating Committee which will have the task of raising funds, training patriots "in all sectors" from the countries concerned, and raising volunteers in each state to help "the various African national liberation movements with the assistance they need in various sectors."

These decisions, as Kenya's Prime Minister, Jomo Kenyatta, has said, mean that "a sentence of death has been passed on colonialism, and a means for executing it have been devised. A greater part of Africa is already free: the Addis Ababa Conference has decreed that the whole of it shall be free."

Other resolutions adopted at the conference were: on Racial Discrimination and Apartheid; on the United Nations; on General Disarmament, and on Economic Co-operation between African States.

The resolution on General Disarmament is of special interest and importance. It includes the declaration of Africa as a nuclear-free zone; the destruction of existing nuclear weapons; the removal of military bases from Africa and the disentanglement of African countries from military pacts with non-African powers; and an appeal to the great powers to reduce conventional weapons, end the arms race, and sign a general and complete disarmament agreement under strict and effective international control.

* * *

The five months since Addis Ababa have been a period in which a difficult struggle has been waged to carry forward the spirit and decisions of the conference. Some successes have been registered; but there have been setbacks, too, and some new obstacles have arisen.

First, the successes. The Co-ordinating Committee to assist these countries still under foreign rule has been set up, and funds are being raised.

Second, as regards Southern Rhodesia, the Portuguese-held territories and South Africa, the concerted efforts of the African states, with the backing of Asian states, the socialist countries, and most European countries, have been able to secure the passing of important resolutions at the United Nations by huge majorities, sometimes only with the small number of Western imperialist states and their supporters voting against.

The adoption (October 11, 1963) at the United Nations General Assembly, by 106 votes for, no abstentions, and only one vote—that of South Africa—against, of a motion condemning the South African government for its "repression of persons opposed to apartheid" and requesting it "to abandon forthwith the arbitrary trial now in progress (of the African leaders) and forthwith to grant unconditional release to all political prisoners and to all persons imprisoned, interned, or subjected to other restrictions for having opposed the policy of apartheid" is a measure of the progress being made.

The actions and demonstrations against South Africa at this year's I.L.O. conference, at the international conference on public education at Geneva, at the United Nations and in a number of other international bodies, are also due to the united pressure of the African states. These states have taken other measures, including, in some cases, stepping up moves for economic sanctions, and denying South Africa landing or fly-over rights for their civil aircraft.

The African Foreign Ministers' Conference, held at Dakar in August 1963, also carried forward the decisions of Addis Ababa with the passing of a resolution inviting all African governments to sign the Moscow Test Ban Treaty, an invitation which has been swiftly followed up by the African states concerned.

On the trade union front, agreement has been reached between representatives of the All-African Trade Union Federation and the African Trade Union Confederation to establish one united trade union federation for the whole of Africa, which would embrace some three million organised workers.

All these advances are being carried forward in the face of new manoeuvres by the imperialists and in an atmosphere in which new divisions could arise. It has to be said that the decisions of the Addis Ababa Conference were not sincerely welcomed in all political circles in Africa. There are some states which still put their own regional or other forms of association above that of full African unity—for example, the Union of African and Malagasy States, the African states associated with the European Common Market, the proposals of President Senghor of Senegal for a new regionalisation of West Africa into three groupings. All these divisive trends are being encouraged by the imperialists.

Equally serious is the fact that the Committee of Nine, or Co-ordinating Committee, set up at Dar-es-Salaam to assist the liberation of the remaining areas of foreign rule in Africa, has not yet been able to respond in the way the peoples of these areas expect. Criticisms have been raised by some of the national movements over the methods adopted by the Committee, in particular its tendency to influence negatively the political developments within the national movements, as well as its preference to spending most of its funds on administration and propaganda *outside* the foreign-dominated territories rather than on more direct assistance to the struggle of the peoples *inside* these territories.

Such weaknesses in the situation, however, are temporary, for the African people are in no mood to tolerate the continuance of colonialism, nor the new manoeuvres of neo-colonialism.

Recent events show that the African revolution is continuing its upward path. The overthrow of the Youlou Government in Congo (Brazzaville) and of the Maga Government in Dahomey, in both cases after mass demonstrations by the workers and trade unions, shows that African governments which fail to respond to the needs and demands of the people and which compromise with imperialism can have no stability in present-day conditions in Africa. Similar recent actions by workers and trade unions in Congo (Leopoldville) and in Senegal, though temporarily suppressed, show again, as does the powerful general strike in Nigeria in October, that the ground is burning under the feet of the compromisers.

Africa is entering a new stage of its revolution, a stage which will be marked by three major characteristics. First, there will be a more intense fight to liberate the remaining territories under foreign rule—a fight in which the peoples still under oppression will be helped by those in the independent African states, as well as by stronger international support. Second, we will see the carrying forward by the most progressive African states of the struggle to reconstruct their economies and to complete the liberation of their countries. And third, a new round of battles is inevitable between the African people and those African governments which are under the influence of neo-colonialism and which try to prevent the people from carrying through a thorough-going national democratic revolution.

Immense difficulties still lie ahead, and there will undoubtedly be further setbacks. But a new world is being born, and Africa is determined to be part of it. Africa is increasingly conscious that she is part of a world turning from capitalism to socialism, and hence that her final victory over imperialism is assured.

JACK WODDIS

London, November 7, 1963

CONTENTS

ERRATA

p. 30, 3rd para., line 7: Read "1892" instead of "1897."
line 10: Read "seven years later" instead of "a year later."

p. 36, 2nd para. of quotation, 1st line: Read "principal characteristic" instead of "principle characteristic."

p. 126, 9th line from bottom: last word of line should be "beside" instead of "side."

The correct spelling is Sekou Touré, not Toure, as it appears in several places.

INTRODUCTION

When the first Conference of Independent African States was held in Accra in 1958 there were eight such states. Today there are thirty-three, and their populations total over 200 million. The tide of independence has swept over most of the continent, leaving only the Spanish-held territories in the north-west, Gambia, Angola and some smaller Portuguese colonies in the west, Kenya, Zanzibar and Mozambique in the east, the two Rhodesias and Nyasaland in the centre, and South West Africa, Swaziland, Basutoland, Bechuanaland and the Republic of South Africa in the remaining southern part. Thus some 50 million African people still languish under European rule.

No African peoples have gained their independence without struggle. They struggled after the Treaty of Berlin in 1885 to prevent their lands falling to the imperialist invaders; they struggled for decades against the effects and consequences of imperialist rule; and they struggled hard for national independence. In some territories the conflict was fiercer than in others. Sometimes the relatively peaceful transfer of power concealed the bitter strife which had preceded it at an earlier stage. But nowhere did the occupying imperialist power voluntarily and of its own free will surrender its strategic bases, economic investments and political privileges and dominance.

It cannot escape one that in the past decade the conflict has been most intense where white settlement has been greatest. Not only has West Africa experienced a quicker and relatively less bloody path to independence than the East, but even in East Africa itself one can see the same pattern. Thus Tanganyika, with 28,000 Europeans, has gained independence more easily than Kenya, with its 58,000 Europeans. Nyasaland, with only 7,000 Europeans, is nearer to independence than Northern

Rhodesia with 66,000, which, in turn, is likely to have a slightly less bloody passage to freedom than Southern Rhodesia, with 250,000 Europeans. Even in the fascist-held Portuguese territories, the conditions of struggle in Mozambique, with 66,000 Europeans, are slightly easier than in Angola, with 200,000. The fierce struggles in Algeria (possessing the largest French settlement, and being the last but one[1] French colony in Africa to win its independence) and in the Congo (also with a large settler population) again illustrate the general truth. And no one will seriously doubt that it is above all in the Republic of South Africa, with its $3\frac{1}{2}$ million Europeans, that the sharpest clash of all is likely to be witnessed.

It is ironic that it is precisely where there are the highest number of Europeans to make good the imperialist claim of a "civilising mission", of "preparing the African people for independence", that the people are, in fact, furthest away from their goal of freedom. Far from European influence being a factor to guide and train Africans for independent government, it is clearly a major stumbling block to such advance. In fact, history has provided a simple arithmetical formula: the greater the number of European settlers, the slower the advance of the Africans to independence. Little wonder that the African people, in their wisdom, have concluded that if they are to make progress then European domination must be ended.

The southern half of Africa which remains to win its independence is directly or indirectly a British responsibility. Most of the territories still suffering under colonial status are in the British Commonwealth, or, like the Republic of South Africa, a creation of British imperialism which is still its mainstay. Portugal, too, is "our oldest ally", and its colonies in Angola, Mozambique, Portuguese Guinea, Cape Verde, Sao Tome, Principe and Cabinda owe much to British economic, political, diplomatic and military support.

A further characteristic of many of these territories which are not yet independent is that they include the main centres of western investments, especially British and American, which tend to flow to the great concentrations of mineral wealth in the Republic of South Africa and the Rhodesias. It is almost inevitable that some of the fiercest battles to liberate Africa are

[1] French Somaliland has not yet won its independence.

yet to come. The Rhodesias, Kenya, the Spanish and Portuguese-held territories—these are likely to be the scene of intense struggle. Some of them have, indeed, already become so.

Thus the great advances made by the African peoples in the past few years, and the ending of direct colonial rule over most of Africa, are in no sense a final victory. Even those states which have won political independence have taken only the first step. Before them lies the important battle to enlarge their area of freedom, to consolidate their political gains and to win their struggle for economic independence and growth. They will be doing this in the face of intense opposition from imperialism which, despite its neo-colonialist face, is ever ready to use the most brutal force and duplicity to hold on to the realities of economic and political power, as it has demonstrated all too clearly in the Congo.

Writing at the end of 1962, one can already see the out-lines of 1963 and beyond. Despite imperialism, further independent African states will arise. The centre of attention will shift more and more, as indeed it has already begun to, to the problems of completing independence, of building independent national democracies, even of advancing towards socialism.

This will be no easy phase for Africa. She will be carrying through her immense task of reconstruction against strong imperialist opposition and in the course of grappling with a series of complex and, in some ways, new problems. How Africa is to face these tasks, what are the views of her parties and leaders, what is there distinctive and new in the African situation, and to what extent do the experiences of other continents have any validity for Africa—these are the matters which constitute the main subject-matter of this book.

There may be some who think more attention should be given to the current struggles to end colonialism in the southern, central and eastern regions of Africa. But a book cannot compete with day-to-day events. And added to the normal delays associated with book-publishing one must take account of the rapidity with which developments in Africa are taking place. Between the first and final drafts of this introduction—itself written after the book proper—three new states came into being, and the date of the fourth was fixed. I have no doubt that by the time this appears in print there will be additional African states. For these reasons this book concentrates on the new Africa arising and on the questions which, more and more, are shifting to the centre of the African scene.

This book is in no sense an attempt to outline a policy for the African people; still less an endeavour to prophesy in detail what will come to pass on the African continent in the next decade or so. It has a far more modest purpose: to indicate the problems the Africans are already facing, and to analyse the attitude taken towards these problems by the African people, their organisations and leading thinkers and statesmen, especially in so far as they show the path which Africa is likely to travel in the coming period.

To many of Africa's problems there can be no absolute and final answer at this stage. And in any case that answer can be given, in the last resort, only by the African people themselves.

This book is intended as a contribution to discussion—a discussion which is already involving people not only in Africa but in all countries wherever men and women are concerned with Africa's fate. In some cases this concern springs from motives of self-interest, out of anxiety to "keep Africa with the West". The present book has no such interest at heart. It is dedicated to the cause of African independence, democracy, peace and prosperity. And it is in loyalty to those aims that it has been written.

December 1962

CHAPTER ONE

CAN AFRICA TAKE A NON-CAPITALIST ROAD?

It is inevitable that with most of Africa free from direct colonial rule there should be widespread discussion taking place on the next steps to be taken after political independence. How are the new African states to build up their economies? What changes are needed in their social and state structure? Will the new Africa be capitalist or socialist? Or neither? Is it possible for Africa to avoid the normal capitalist stage, and pass straight through to socialism? Or must Africa tread the path of the western world, experience the long, painful haul of capitalism as an inevitable phase in her development?

In general it can be said that the overwhelming majority of African national parties, their leaders and the new governments have declared themselves in favour of a "socialist" way forward, and have rejected "capitalism", which is regarded, quite understandably, as the handiwork of the enemy who oppressed them for so long. Imperialism, colonialism, neo-colonialism, capitalism —all are condemned equally by the awakened people of Africa. Many conceptions of "socialism" are being put forward, and, as we shall see, some of them are of very dubious origin. Nevertheless, the popularity of socialism and the tendency to reject capitalism, even if not always fully grounded on scientific understanding, are powerful subjective factors which can play an important role in assisting Africa to avoid the stage of full capitalist development.

The new African states, in their present stage, are not normal capitalist societies. Hundreds of years of slavery and robbery, and sixty years of imperialist domination, have stunted and distorted normal economic growth, delayed and restricted class formation. As a result, African capitalism has never been fully developed. All the key points in the economy of the African colonies were held by imperialist monopolies, and only as an exception was an indigenous African capitalist class able to emerge. This was limited mainly to trade, and even within this limitation was a significant development only in parts of West Africa, and in Uganda, where white settlement was inconsiderable. Elsewhere, an African capitalist class scarcely exists; and even in Nigeria or the Ivory Coast, where a more substantial African bourgeoisie is developing, it is still not a powerful factory-owning, monopoly bourgeoisie, but a class which is relatively weak in relation to imperialism on which it therefore is still largely dependent.

Can the new African states, under these conditions, take the normal capitalist road of development? Leaving aside for the moment the question of the African workers and peasants and the road they might decide to take, the passing into the full stage of capitalist development in Africa seems most unlikely. The experience of Latin America shows that relatively weak, nominally independent states which still belong to the capitalist world system inevitably are dominated by more powerful capitalist states, by imperialist states, and in consequence the semi-feudal, agrarian character of the weaker states is largely preserved and their full capitalist development held back. If the new African states try to take the capitalist road, that is to say, remain as part of the capitalist system, then inevitably they will be dependent on imperialism and will be prevented from development as fully capitalist states. As capitalist states, the African countries could make a challenge to imperialism only if they, too, became powerful imperialist states, passed into the phase of monopoly capitalism on the basis of a powerful modern industry, and in economic, military and political power became strong enough to stand up to United States imperialism or British imperialism. But such a "normal" development of the new African states into modern imperialist states is inconceivable. In the first place, the existing imperialist powers will not allow it. Secondly, the workers and peasants in the independent African states will not allow it. And, lastly, the international relation of class forces, the present stage of world development, precludes it.

Africa, in short, is too late to go through the process of full capitalist development. The world is turning from capitalism to socialism, and Africa, as part of this historic world process, will turn likewise.

If the independent African states are, historically speaking, precluded from full capitalist development only two paths are left to them. Either they attempt to take a capitalist path, and in so doing both cling to imperialism as a protector against the forces of socialism and, at the same time, struggle against imperialism as the barrier to African capitalism—and this is a path strewn with contradictions and obstacles which can end only in dragging Africa through the morass of capitalism in decline. Or they can reject the capitalist path altogether.

In the first case the only fate in store for the African states would be that suffered by the independent states of Latin America—independent in name, trying to follow a capitalist path, but in fact completely dependent on imperialism with, in consequence, all progressive development throttled. Feudalism, illiteracy, disease and stifling dictatorships—that is the end of former colonies in Latin America striving to take the capitalist road. A total of 120 million persons suffering from chronic under-nourishment; 140 million illiterates; an average expectation of life of thirty-five years; millions of children dying before they learn to walk; grave disease and mass epidemics; millions of landless peasants and a handful of great landowners; miserable wages and mass unemployment and $1,500 million drained off to the United States each year in profits. Such has been the fate of Latin America. And such, too, would be the fate of Africa. The Nkrumahs, Kenyattas, Sekou Toures, Keitas and Luthulis would be swept aside—and the Tshombes, Kasavubus, Mobutus, Busias and Gbedemahs would take their place.

Africa, if she is to progress, is bound to take a non-capitalist road. Such a road does not preclude, for a time, a capitalist sector of the economy. In fact, African states can take a non-capitalist road and still allow—for a transitional period—a sphere of their economy in capitalist hands, both private and state, national and foreign. After all, the Soviet Union allowed, for a time, the continuation of private capitalism, and even encouraged it under the New Economic Policy; and for a time certain concessions were offered to foreign capital under which it was allowed its profits but had to observe Soviet labour laws. The decisive question was the policy of the government, the direction in which the country was moving. The Soviet Government, based on the power of the workers and peasants, had the commanding positions in its hands and could therefore guide society in a socialist direction.

Similarly, any African state which is determined to follow a non-capitalist road, and is consciously directing its whole resources towards that goal, can tolerate for a time a capitalist sector in its economy—even foreign capital—as long as it takes ever firmer steps to restrict and confine (and eventually eliminate) that sector while putting increasing emphasis on the state sector of the economy. Taking the non-capitalist path, after all, is a transitional phase, a phase in which state forms, political organs and economic structure will all be transitional. A state taking a non-capitalist road is not a state taking some third path, a path neither capitalist nor socialist, a path leading to some unknown "third goal". It is a state which is travelling in a most decided direction *away* from capitalism and *towards* socialism. The non-capitalist path is not a new form of society but, as the term should make clear, a direction that society is taking.

To travel such a road is by no means a new conception. This was the road travelled by the former colonies of tsarist Russia. It was the road travelled by the Mongolian People's Republic, which in forty years transformed its nomadic society and passed through from its stage of elementary feudalism to socialism without so much as a breath of capitalism sweeping over the land.[1] It was the road being travelled by the People's Republic of Vietnam, the People's Democratic Republic of Korea and the People's Republic of China.

What is Socialism?

But one can travel a non-capitalist road only if one is clear as to the nature of capitalism and socialism. Some of the theories at

---

[1] Mongolia did not complete its first, anti-feudal stage until as late as 1940, by which time there were still less than 15,000 industrial workers in a population of one million.

present being put forward regarding socialism in Africa and Asia are by no means scientific. At present, in all the newly developing states there is talk of "socialism". Sometimes it is "co-operative socialism", sometimes "traditional socialism", sometimes it is "democratic socialism"—as if there were another form of socialism which was not democratic. There is even talk in Morocco of "Muslim socialism", and in Egypt of "Arab socialism" and the "socialism of Islam".

In a recent article Emile Bustani argues that all Arab countries are "consciously drifting towards some form of socialism". (*New Statesman*, 5 January 1962.) But when one reads on to learn what form of "socialism" these states are strangely "drifting" towards, one is told that "Forms of socialism differ. Even under its present Tory government Britain is a model Socialist state in comparison with any country in the Middle East." It then turns out that for Emile Bustani "socialism" is simply welfare, and evidently does not include the abolition of private capitalism. In fact, he says that "my own Lebanon is turning towards Socialism" and then adds that "it is unthinkable to any Lebanese that private enterprise should be abolished". In other words, on examination, this theory of "socialism" is found to be none other than the mixed economy so beloved of right-wing Labour leaders. There are some theoreticians who argue in this same way as regards future developments in Africa.

A quite different kind of argument is used by Leopold Senghor, President of Senegal. He boldly asserts "we have no intention of retaining capitalism, not in its nineteenth century form at least", but then proceeds to argue that African society is

"traditionally *socialist* in character. In this sense, that our Negro-African society is a classless society, which is not the same as saying that it has no hierarchy or division of labour. It is a *community-based society*. . . . Thus, in the working out of our African Mode of Socialism, the problem is not how to put an end to the exploitation of man by his fellow, but to prevent it ever happening. . . ."

Having thus abolished the exploitation of man by man in these words, Leopold Senghor then continues illogically: "And yet we have not legally suppressed capitalism which is foreign to our country; we have not even nationalised anything." In other words, despite his earlier statement, he is forced, in effect, to admit that, whatever the past, Senegal today is *not* a classless society, and, further, that Senegal still has to contend with the existence of private capital, including large-scale foreign capital. Thus, despite what Leopold Senghor says, the problem is indeed not how to prevent the exploitation of man by man *"ever happening"* but how to *"put an end"* to it.

It is true that in Africa's pre-colonial past, at a time when primitive communal society was the general pattern, certain "community-based" characteristics were present. And, as we shall see, certain of these characteristics, which still exist, can help to carry Africa forward along a non-capitalist road. But twentieth-century Africa cannot return to her traditional past—and of course Leopold Senghor himself is fully aware of this. But by emphasising Africa's "traditional socialism" in this way he avoids closer study and decision as to what Africa must do *now*, what precise steps it must take to abolish the exploitation of man by man and build a socialist society.

Like Leopold Senghor, Tanganyika's president, Julius Nyerere, argues that traditional African society was socialist.

> "Nobody starved, either of food or human dignity, because he lacked personal wealth; he could depend on the wealth possessed by the community of which he was a member. That was Socialism." (*The Basis of African Socialism.*)

Nyerere therefore draws the conclusion that the basic difference between socialism and capitalism "does not lie in their methods of producing wealth, but in the way that wealth is distributed". In arguing thus, Nyerere not only ignores the fact that capitalism is based on the exploitation of man by man and that the exploitation takes place in production, in "producing wealth", but he fails to explain the main characteristics of traditional African society. The African peoples, like peoples elsewhere, went through a stage of primitive communal society. The essence of that society was that *there was no private ownership of the means of production; ownership was communal, work was collective, no man exploited another, there were no classes*—and that was why distribution tended to be on the basis of man's needs, and no man ate while another starved, nor did anyone enrich himself at another's expense.

But in Africa today, even though many traditions of primitive communal society still exist in attenuated or sometimes distorted form, class society is developing and, furthermore, the African people are still exploited by the big foreign monopolies which control much of Africa's wealth. Socialism cannot be said to exist while private ownership (foreign or domestic) of the means of production continues to predominate in the economy of Africa.

This underlines the significance of Kwame Nkrumah's correct emphasis that "socialism assumes the public ownership of the means of production—the land and its resources—and the use of these means of production that will bring benefit to the people". (Address to the Accra Study Group of the Convention People's Party, 22 April, 1961.)

Of course, the *paths* to socialism and the *forms* it will take in the African countries will differ, in many respects, from those of the Soviet Union, Eastern Europe, Asia or Cuba. They will naturally draw to the full on the history, traditions, culture, institutions and customs of the African people. But experience shows that in addition to the variations in the way socialism is achieved and the forms it takes, there are certain basic laws of the development of socialism which, taken in their general aspect, are valid for all countries passing from capitalism to socialism.

This is fully recognised by the most advanced political thinkers in the African national movements. Thus the Ghanaian weekly journal *The Spark* comments in its editorial of 29 December 1962:

"Socialist orientation does not mean preaching a hotchpotch of pragmatism-cum-humanism-cum-metaphysics plastered over with idiosyncrasies and passed off as African socialism. African socialism can mean no more than the basic tenets of socialism in an African setting. It means the evolution of African forms and institutions for translating into a working reality the quintessence of socialism which is universal in its validity."

Here is a clear recognition that overriding the differences in forms and institutions are general laws of the transition from

capitalism to socialism which have a general application everywhere.

What are these laws? First, that to build socialism political
power must be in the hands of the working people, the workers,
peasants and intelligentsia, and that this democratic power must
be guided by the working class, since this is the class which is
directly connected with industry, the material base on which
socialism rests. It is the working class which, because of its
position in society, is the most highly organised and best able to
act as an organised force; the class which, by virtue of the natural
development of society, is the growing class; and the only class
which, because it possesses nothing but its own labour power,
can without hesitation embrace the idea of the public ownership
of the means of production since it has nothing to lose but its
chains of capitalist exploitation.

Secondly, that to achieve socialism, the working class has to
rally around itself all the progressive forces in society. In underdeveloped regions as Africa this means above all uniting with
the peasantry who comprise the overwhelming majority of the
population. The alliance of the working class and the peasantry
will provide the bedrock on which the unity of all progressive
forces will be based.

Thirdly, that to ensure that political power is in the hands of
the people guided by the working class it is not enough to enjoy
universal franchise and other election rights, and to be able to
exercise democratic freedoms; the key is to wield state power, to
direct the whole apparatus of government and state, including
the armed forces and the police which, if left in the hands of pro-
imperialist or capitalist forces, can be turned against the workers
and peasants, and their organisations. The first step in effecting
this change in the control of the state in Africa is the struggle for
Africanisation, that is, to clear out the remaining cadres of
imperialism from the state apparatus; but this is only a first
step, which must be followed by a change in the *class* character
of the state if progress is to be made towards socialism.

Fourthly, that the political power of the working people must
be used to transform all the means of production—factories,
mines, land, banks, transport and other enterprises—into collective property, the property of the whole people, so that no man
can exploit the labour of another, no man employ another in

order to make profit from his labour. This collective property can take differing forms: ownership by the state, ownership by local councils or ownership by groups of people or co-operatives.

There is no place in such a society for the private landlord or private employer. Individual farmers, or traders, shopkeepers, craftsmen may continue, if they wish—but only if they work on their own account; not if they exploit the labour of others. And this would apply also to those who are not themselves private employers but who hold shares in private firms. With the taking over, by the people, of such enterprises, the capitalist shareholders would have to surrender their stranglehold on the economy.

Fifthly, with the means of production in the hands of the people, and with the decisive sections of the economy in the hands of the state, production can be planned instead of being left to the anarchy of private profit interests; and, further, the main aim of production becomes that of satisfying the material and spiritual needs of the people and no longer that of filling the pockets of private capitalists, whether foreign or indigenous.

To carry through this great transformation of society, especially in a continent like Africa which has been so terribly ravaged by imperialism for sixty years, requires enormous effort. Difficult as is the struggle to end colonial rule, the struggle to build a new Africa along socialist lines is still far more difficult. Not only is it necessary to carry through this great change in the face of constant opposition and sabotage by the forces of international imperialism, allied with the forces of internal reaction—feudal and tribal leaders, career politicians who are hangers-on of imperialism, local capitalists who think more of their pockets and privileges than of the national interest. Equally one must overcome the people's force of habit, this "terrible force", as Lenin termed it, which continues long after the original conditions which gave rise to it have gone. In Africa this means a struggle against tribalism, against petty parochial ideas, against superstitions of all kinds, against the self-centred ideas of the small producer or farmer, against a contemptuous attitude towards women— against the whole range of ideas and habits of thought which hold man in thrall, stifle his initiative, keep him in ignorance, rob him of confidence and prevent him from utilising his great potential creative power in the interests of the whole people.

It is precisely to contend with such difficulties that the working class needs to establish its own leading role, to use the power of the state to guide the whole people in the building of a new life. The state is not merely a weapon to safeguard the new people's power and crush the enemy; it is even more a powerful educative and constructive weapon to enable men to transform society and thus, in the process, transform themselves.

One can readily see what a heavy and difficult responsibility rests on the back of the working class. Such a historic task can be performed only by a class which has a body of scientific theory, a theory based on the experience of the struggle for socialism throughout the world, from which general laws of universal validity have been established. Such a science is Marxism-Leninism; and to wield this weapon the working class must be organised *politically*, must have the possibility of championing its own political viewpoint.

The absence of such an organisation is one of the main factors holding back Africa from taking a non-capitalist path, and thus leaving her still a prey to imperialist influences—political, ideological, economic and military. If Africa is to take the leap upwards from her present stage towards socialism, then a number of other problems and weaknesses must also be overcome. There is the disunity within some territories, based sometimes on tribalism, sometimes on the petty ambitions of individual leaders of different parties or even within the same party. There is disunity and friction, too, between different African territories, arising partly from the artificial boundaries left by the imperialist division of Africa, partly from the strivings of the national bourgeoisie with their aims of expanding their "own" territory, strivings which are inflamed and utilised all the time by imperialism, which is naturally interested in setting the African people at loggerheads so as to maintain its own dominant position. There is, too, a lack of organisation amongst the peasantry, even though there has been some development of co-operatives; but these organisations are often limited in scope, and in no sense fully developed vehicles by which the peasants can express and work for their demands. Many of the workers, too, are only of the present generation, return frequently to their villages, and thus do not yet provide that solid, permanent proletarian base on which a Marxist-Leninist organisation could be built, and so make possible the formation of a worker-peasant alliance, the real basis for national unity and for the advance towards socialism.

For all these reasons the possibility of the new African states taking the non-capitalist path of development and moving towards socialism does not mean that it will be easy for these states to take such a path. It will, in fact, require an extraordinary effort by the whole people, and will demand, too, outstanding leadership, clear-sightedness and courage.

Weakness of the African Capitalist Class

Yet, at the same time, the newly developing African states have a number of factors in their favour. First, as we have noticed, the national bourgeoisie is extremely weak in most territories, and nowhere is it a powerful class, certainly not as strong as the bourgeoisie was in pre-independent India or China. Before 1947 there were already large factory-owning groups of Indian capitalists, such as Tata and Birla, who were beginning, even at that stage, to spread their links both vertically and horizontally, securing a strong position in entire industries and extending their influence through a whole range of enterprises. In China, too, prior to 1949, there were Chinese capitalists owning large factories, as, for example, the textile-factory owners in Shanghai. In Africa the bourgeoisie is not only relatively weak; it is also, in the main, a much newer class than the working class. The African proletariat was called into being by imperialism at the turn of the century. Throughout these sixty-odd years the African working class has grown numerically, become more of a modern industrial proletariat, conducted big mass struggles and strikes against imperialism, formed trade unions and taken part in political activity. It is, in many ways, an experienced working class, although it is still handicapped by its lack of Marxist clarity. But the African bourgeoisie lacks experience. It is a new class economically, and certainly lacks political experience in government, in maintaining its influence and domination over the workers and peasants as well as in preserving national sovereignty in the face of new pressures and plots from imperialists.

As a class, the African bourgeoisie lacks experience in the

industrial field too. This partly explains its preferring to continue to make its profits in the familiar fields of trade and farming, in speculation and property, and even by investing in
European enterprises, rather than tie up its capital in its own
factory development. One consequence of this is to leave industrial development to foreign monopolies.

But, on the other hand, the unwillingness of African private
capital to develop industry is compelling the new African states
to intervene and take energetic and decisive steps to develop
state industry. This, of course, is not the only reason why these
states are building up their own state sector of the economy.
The African bourgeoisie, apart from its lack of experience, is
just not powerful enough economically, is not rich enough, to be
able to finance such great projects as the Tema Harbour or the
Volta Dam in Ghana, the Niger Dam in Nigeria, or similar
important constructions which are being planned in Mali,
Guinea and other states. The western powers are not always
prepared to loan funds for such projects which can strengthen
economic independence, and are rarely prepared to invest in
them either. Consequently, the new African states have found it
necessary to look towards a state sector of the economy as an
important means of economic development, very often with the
aid of loans and technical assistance and equipment from the
socialist countries.

The net result of all this is that instead of a rapidly growing
private sector in a number of African territories we see the growing importance of state enterprise, with the state taking the
initiative in building up industry and in stimulating economic
growth in general. It is possible that in some African states this
state sector of the economy, a form of national development,
will become the predominant factor in the national economy.
This can facilitate the taking of a non-capitalist path in such
states, provided that the workers and peasants increasingly
exercise their influence on governmental policy and advance
towards the guidance of these states.

It might be argued that these developments should not be
exaggerated; that, in effect, they are only a form of state capitalism. But as distinct from the state monopoly capitalism of the
imperialist countries, the state sector of the economy in the independent African states plays a role as an instrument of national

growth and against imperialist domination. Furthermore, decisive political and state changes could take place in these countries which would strengthen the people's democratic control over the nation's economy and thus facilitate the taking of a non-capitalist path.

In some African states, as for example Ghana, Guinea, Mali and Tanganyika, it would be wrong to say simply that these states are led by the national bourgeoisie, and leave it at that. In actual fact, especially in Guinea, Mali and Tanganyika, the African capitalist class is extremely weak. Owing to the way Africa has developed in the colonial epoch, the national movements in these countries were led, in the main, by representatives of the intelligentsia together with leaders of the trade unions and the working-class movement. Men like Nkrumah, Sekou Toure, Modibo Keita, Julius Nyerere are not themselves big capitalists, but members of the intelligentsia. They are patriotic democrats; and there are other such patriots alongside them. This does not mean, however, that these states represent the economic power of the intelligentsia, nor that it is the political power of the intelligentsia which rules. Lenin once pointed out that the intelligentsia "is not an *independent* economic class and therefore does not represent any *independent* political force". (Lenin: *Collected Works*, Vol. II, p. 380.) It would be idle, therefore, to assert that the intelligentsia are "in power" in such states. Such a thing is not possible.

In many independent African states it is unmistakably clear that African bourgeois forces are in power, usually in alliance with feudal chiefs. But in some states patriotic democrats, leaning on working-class support, are able to limit the activities of the new capitalist class and reduce the power of the chiefs. These patriotic democrats, representatives of the intelligentsia, are sometimes influenced by the ideas of the new, weak, yet growing capitalist class. But this leadership is not only subject, by education, circumstances, external pressure and so on, to bourgeois influences; it is also subject to the pressure of its own workers and peasants who are increasingly embracing socialist ideas. In addition, Africa's most outstanding leaders are also influenced by world developments; they have learnt much from the failures and crimes of imperialism, as well as from the successes and disinterested help of the socialist countries. Some of them have studied Marxism, and have found that it helps them to find solutions to their country's problems. These leaders are capable, talented men, men of vision and intelligence, with a basic desire to destroy all the hangovers of colonialism and to help Africa rise to her full stature, free, independent, enlightened, proud and prosperous. History shows that such men, with their country's interests at heart, can rise above the views and interests of the capitalist class, can ally themselves with the working class, and help forward their country's progress. One can cite the example of Sun Yat-sen, that great Chinese patriot and democrat, who in his last days urged the Chinese people to co-operate with the Soviet Union, and called on his Kuomintang Party (at that time progressive) to co-operate with the Communist Party. In our own day we have seen Fidel Castro, a great revolutionary leader, fully embracing Marxism-Leninism and emerging not only as a national figure but as a clear-sighted fighter for socialism too. Castro is not an exceptional Cuban phenomenon; exceptional he certainly is, but the path he has taken will yet be taken in other countries by similar patriots and revolutionary heroes.

Thus, the class structure of Africa and the times we live in create certain favourable factors for Africa to take a non-capitalist path. The very weakness of the national bourgeoisie in Africa has compelled the imperialists, at this late stage in history, to try to foster such a class, or at least what they term "an African middle class"—that is, a stratum of African capitalist farmers (or *kulaks*), of well-paid (or bribed) African politicians, with ministerial posts of £3,000 a year and more, and of participants in European monopoly firms, even as directors of such firms, in order to create a social class which will be favourable to a *capitalist* path of development in collaboration with imperialism. While certain groups and individuals might be won to the side of imperialism by these manœuvres, history is not on the side of the imperialists. For decades they stifled all normal capitalist development in Africa, robbed the African people and prevented the capital accumulated in Africa being used to serve African interests. Their late and desperate efforts to foster an African "middle class" as an ally of imperialism may meet with some temporary successes and place obstacles in the way of Africa's progress; but they cannot prevent the further disintegration of the colonial system in Africa and the growing demand of the African people that imperialism be uprooted completely.

"If we look the facts in the face," Khrushchov has said, "we shall have to admit that the imperialists have powerful economic levers with which to exert pressure on the newly independent countries. They still succeed in enmeshing some of the politically independent countries in the web of economic dependence. . . .

But if we take account of all the factors shaping the destinies of the peoples that have shaken off colonial rule, we will see that in the final analysis the trends of social progress opposing imperialism are bound to prevail."

(Speech *For New Victories for the World Communist Movement* by N. S. Khrushchov, 6 January 1961, reporting on the meeting of the 81 Communist and Workers' Parties.)

Africa's Land Problems

There is another factor in Africa which can assist her in taking a non-capitalist path and finding the way to socialism, and that is the character of the land problem. In brief one can say that in most of Africa south of the Sahara the pattern on the land is as follows.

First, the existence of large European plantations on which Africans work, usually on a seasonal basis, for wages; and, along with such plantations, European farms in the areas of white settlement—Kenya, Northern and Southern Rhodesia, the Republic of South Africa, Angola and Mozambique, South West Africa and a few other territories. All this comprises a sector of European-owned capitalist agriculture.

Secondly, the existence of African capitalist farmers growing cash crops mainly for export, and ranging from large African-owned rubber farms in Liberia, substantial African farmers in Ghana, Nigeria, Ivory Coast and Uganda, to the small cash-crop farmers who have emerged, especially in the past five years, in Kenya, the Rhodesias and Nyasaland, and Tanganyika, or who have existed for some time in West Africa and Uganda.

Thirdly, the majority of African peasants, who live on communally owned land, carrying on subsistence farming or, in some cases, combining this with growing cash crops both for the internal market and for export.

Fourthly, although there is feudalism in parts of Africa, as for instance in Northern Nigeria and in Uganda, it would be entirely erroneous to think that the main problem on the land in Africa is that of feudalism. In tropical Africa the struggle against feudal landlordism, against feudal rent, high interest rates, indebtedness and mass evictions from the land through failure to meet debt, interest and rent obligations to the feudal landlord-cum-moneylender is not the main content of the land question as it is in Asia. And that is why in the programmes of African parties and trade unions, or in the declarations and resolutions of the All-African Peoples Conference, such questions are not raised. The main robber of African land is not, as has been the case in Asia, the large feudal landlord, but rather the large foreign monopolies which have seized valuable mineral-bearing land and have established large-scale plantations for cash crops, and the white settlers who have seized the best land for capitalist farming. And the main exploiter of the African peasant is not the feudal landlord of Asia, often taking as much as 60 per cent of the peasant's crop as rent and charging 100 per cent interest on loans to meet this rent, but the plantation companies who compete against the African peasant-producer on unequal terms, and the big overseas trading monopolies, such as the United Africa Company, which buy up the African peasant's crops at the lowest possible price.

Not that feudal forms of exploitation have no importance in Africa. In many territories—and not only in the north, or in Nigeria and Uganda—feudalism has made headway within the communal land system. In process of time the chief has often been able to acquire, through his authority, a privileged economic position. His power to allocate the common land naturally gives him the possibility of furthering his own interests; and, in addition, the traditional "gifts" to the chief and the "voluntary labour" performed by the peasants for the benefit of the tribe as a whole have become transformed more and more into forms of feudal dues, through which the chiefs have enriched themselves. Nevertheless it would be erroneous to regard feudal exploitation as the main problem for the African peasant. Neither is the exploitation of the poorer peasants by the African capitalist farmers a major consideration yet, although this class is growing and represents a new factor in the situation.

Thus, for Africa (apart from the North where feudalism was well developed prior to the attainment of political independence) the question of agriculture and land reform poses a number of problems different to those which faced the peasants of China, or which now face the peasants of India or Indonesia.

The fact that in most of Africa communally owned land is still the rule has its obvious significance, especially when considering the possibility of a non-capitalist path of development for such countries. Interestingly enough, in those African territories still under British colonial rule, such as Kenya and the Central African Federation, imperialism has in recent years taken steps to break up the former communal land-holdings, to introduce individual title to land and to foster a small stratum of African capitalist farmers in the hope that they will act as a conservative brake on the movement for genuine independence and for radical social and economic change. The consequences of this policy, the dispossession of thousands of peasants who have lost their land to "model farmers", "yeoman farmers" and the like, produce their end result in the large-scale unemployment which is now such a marked feature of towns like Nairobi in Kenya, or Bulawayo and Harare in Southern Rhodesia.

The traditional African form of land tenure, in which there is no individual *ownership* of land, but only individual *use* of commonly owned land, means that, under independent African governments, it should prove possible to carry forward this principle of collective ownership of land, and combine it with collective forms of work, such as pooling machinery and the collective marketing of products. The existence of marketing co-operatives in many parts of Africa (even though in many cases they were encouraged and supervised by colonial governments and big foreign monopolies as a means of controlling the peasants, purchasing their stocks in bulk without having to establish an elaborate machinery of buying from thousands of individual peasants, and for keeping down prices) can also assist this development, provided that the co-operatives are transformed into genuine organisations of the peasants, controlled by them and able to defend their interests. In this way the existence of commonly owned land can be an important factor facilitating the taking by Africa of a non-capitalist path of development.

It is not without interest that in the nineteenth century Marx and Engels discussed the question as to whether the Russian commune (with its basis in commonly held land) could make possible the transition to socialism without passing through the capitalist stage. In a preface to the Russian edition of the *Communist Manifesto* in 1882 they wrote:

> "The question now is: Can the Russian village commune—a form of primitive communal land ownership which has already to a large extent been destroyed—pass directly to the higher communist form of common ownership? Or, on the contrary, must it first go through the same process of disintegration as that which constituted the historical development of the West? The only possible answer to this question today is as follows: If the Russian Revolution becomes the signal for a workers' revolution in the West, so that one supplements the other, then the present form of common land ownership in Russia may serve as the starting point for a Communist development."

In other words, Marx and Engels did not rule out the possibility, under certain conditions, of the Russian peasant commune being transformed into a socialist form of property. As is well known, the conditions which they had in mind never arose. The "workers' revolution in the West" did not take place, capitalism took root in Russia and spread to the countryside and the commune began to fade away. Already by 1897 Engels had come to the conclusion that there was little possibility of saving Russia from "passing through the torments of the capitalist regime". And a year later Lenin, in his work *The Development of Capitalism in Russia*[1], showed how the development of capitalism had destroyed the traditional basis of the peasant society, but that, in the process, it had weakened feudalism in the countryside, helped to raise the productivity of labour and so brought the Russian peasantry to the threshold of a new stage in its development.

[1] Later, in 1908, in his work *The Agrarian Question in Russia*, Lenin noted "everywhere we observe that the trend of the village commune is towards the peasant bourgeoisie".

Africa in the 1960s has little in common with Russia at the end of the nineteenth century. And the world, too, has moved on considerably in the past sixty years. In Africa itself communally owned land is under attack; capitalism is growing in the African countryside, in the newly independent states as well as in those states still dominated by white settlers. Compared with sixty or even thirty years ago, the significant new phenomenon in the African countryside is the individual African farmer growing cocoa, palm, coffee, cotton, tobacco, tea or rubber as an export crop for cash, and sometimes employing other African labour. These African farmers are not, in any sense, the dominant class in the African countryside, but they are most decidedly a growing class. Differentiation is clearly taking place amongst the African peasantry; a handful are emerging at the top as more prosperous farmers (a *kulak* class in embryo); many more are sandwiched in the middle as peasants who, in most cases, are clinging on to their positions; and, at the bottom, a mass of impoverished peasants are leaving the land in search of jobs, hundreds of thousands joining the new armies of unemployed or partially employed which now throng the cities.

This process is accelerating modifications in the form of land tenure. Dr. T. O. Elias has emphasised that with the introduction of cash economy and the new economic conceptions that accompany it

"Land has . . . acquired, in many urban or semi-urban areas, a money value and this has had far-reaching social consequences. The old limited practices of lending, pledging and leasing land for returns in kind have to some extent given place to mortgaging and leasing land on the English model, even though such dealings are still subject to family consent where the parcel forms part of the family land."

(*Government and Politics in Africa:* Delhi, 1961, p. 182.)

Yet, despite this development, traditional forms of land tenure based on common ownership are still widespread, and in many regions are the dominant form of land ownership. It is therefore possible, if the African states turn rapidly in a socialist direction, that this collective property can be preserved and transformed into fully socialist property which, with the aid of government credits, seed, chemicals and farm machinery, can bring prosperity to the African countryside. The questions of land reform and forms of tenure, of agricultural development and changes in the methods of farming, are still under discussion in Africa. Experience in Guinea and Ghana serves to emphasise the importance of co-operative production, based on the already existing communal lands, as one form of developing agriculture. In Guinea, for example, the village committee has replaced the chief as the body which allocates land for use. The committee now has the responsibility, and the land is under its control. Production is still often individual, but land ownership and the marketing of products is co-operative. In Ghana experiments are being tried under which the village allocates a certain area of its common land to be worked in common, a number of villagers being allocated to spend a specified amount of time on these collective plots. The government itself also helps by providing seed and by loaning machinery and skilled operators. The choice of crop is decided mutually by the government and the village; but the crop, when harvested, belongs to the villagers.

State farms, with Soviet assistance, are also being tried out in Ghana and Guinea; and other African states, such as Somalia, are carrying out similar experiments. Of significance, too, is the fact that in all new African states the governments are encouraging the development of co-operatives in the countryside, in particular with the aim of extending their sphere of activity from being confined only to co-operative marketing to taking up co-operative production.

The taking over of the big foreign plantations and farms is another development that will help Africa to by-pass the normal capitalist stage. This has not yet happened on any considerable scale, but in some places, as in Guinea, some fruit plantations have been taken over and now act as model plantations and research centres.

Admittedly all these new developments are only a beginning, but they indicate certain possibilities which could help to facilitate Africa's taking of a non-capitalist path of development.

Thus there are a number of factors in Africa which, despite the many obstacles, favour Africa taking a non-capitalist path. These favourable factors, as we have seen, are the weakness and lack of experience of the national bourgeoisie, the growing strength of the African working class, the creation and growth of a state sector of the economy, economic planning, the development of co-operatives, economic and technical aid from socialist countries, the existence of traditional forms of communal land tenure, the growing desire of the African people to build a socialist form of society and their decided turn against imperialism, colonialism, neo-colonialism and capitalism. As N. Numade, a leader of the Communist Party of South Africa, has explained:

"The *main* direction of the national liberation movement in Africa is—decidedly and increasingly—democratic, anti-imperialist and anti-capitalist. More and more Africans are coming to understand that we cannot stop short at formal independence and the trappings of Western bourgeois parliamentarism; that if it is to fulfil its goal of emancipating the peoples fully from the accursed heritage of imperialism our Revolution must sweep forward uninterruptedly to accomplish the social transformation of African society.

In this our position differs markedly from that of Europe and America during the bourgeois-democratic revolutions of the eighteenth and nineteenth centuries. There, having achieved power for themselves, the ruling classes turned conservative and reactionary, and the workers and peasants who had fought for freedom found that its benefits were mainly confined to the rich.

This marked difference stems from the character of the period in which we live, as well as from the specific and urgent needs of the African peoples, their class character, their aims and aspirations. . . . Workers, peasants, patriotic intellectuals, small businessmen and professional men, traders and independent craftsmen—such are the overwhelming bulk of the members of the patriotic liberation movements in Africa. None of these groups have a serious vested interest in the maintenance of capitalism."

(*The African Communist:* May 1961.)

A New Phase in Human Development

But not only are there favourable internal factors for Africa
taking a non-capitalist path; there are favourable external
factors, too. We live in an epoch entirely different from that which
existed sixty years ago, when the division of Africa by the big
imperialist powers was more or less completed. The completion
of that carve-up ushered in the imperialist epoch, an epoch in
which the big western powers ruled the roost, the big monopolies carved out their spheres of interest and influence, colonialism dominated the major portion of the globe and the struggles
of the oppressed peoples suffered bloody defeats at the hands of
imperialism. Huge imperialist empires were created—and, in
their insatiate greed for more, these giant powers clashed in their
desperate endeavour to rend still more territory and wealth from
one another. Thus, the first world war of 1914–18 was fought
to redivide the world; and millions of people in Europe, Asia,
Africa and America suffered to make the world safe, not, as it
was claimed by the Entente powers, for "democracy", but for
profits. But the peoples were not prepared to suffer in silence.
At the very birth of this epoch the rumblings could be heard of
the growing anger of the downtrodden millions. The Russian
revolution of 1905, Bambata's rebellion in South Africa in 1906,
the Persian reform movement of 1906, the big movement in
India around Tilak's campaign in 1907, the Mexican revolution
of 1912, the Chilembwe rising in Nyasaland in 1915, the Irish
Easter Rising in 1916—all these were signs of the coming storm.
At last, in October 1917, the thunder-clap came: the Russian
workers and peasants, aided by the millions of oppressed peoples
in the border regions of the tsarist empire, rose in revolt, swept
away the old power of the princes and profiteers, and established,
for the first time in world history, the firm power of the working
people under the leadership of the working class and its Communist party.

This historic victory ushered in a new phase in human development. It was a revolution pledged to eliminate the exploitation
of man by man and, in so doing, to eliminate the exploitation of
nation by nation. Not only did October 1917 place power in the
hands of the working people, take over the factories, land and

banks from the capitalists and landlords, and start the building of socialism. It also liberated the former oppressed people of tsarist Russia, and opened a new page in Russia's relations with exploited nations. The Tsar's unequal treaties were annulled, concession rights which had been exacted from China were abolished, new relations established with neighbouring states, and help given to new states such as Turkey, as well as to Afghanistan. Great as was the influence of these sweeping changes, they were not yet decisive enough to change the character of the epoch, nor to determine the direction in which humanity moved. Modify it they did, but the new forces in the world released by the 1917 October Revolution were not yet sufficient to save Ethiopia in 1935; nor Spain in 1936–9; and imperialism, with relative impunity, could still crush the rising rebellions in India, Indonesia and Indochina and the growing discontent that was breaking out in Africa and the Middle East. But the failure of the joint strength of imperialism to crush the Chinese revolution, which throughout the 1930s went from strength to strength, was a sign of the times—a clear indication of the big changes due to follow and of the new stage into which the world was moving.

The defeat of fascism in the second world war, the setback which this meant for all imperialisms, the experience of the peoples of Africa and Asia in the course of the war, the emergence of the Soviet Union as the leading force in the antifascist victory— all this shook the whole world system of imperialism. First in Indochina, then in Indonesia, then in other Asian countries, the people showed they were determined not to have back their former oppressors. New republics were formed, and in 1947 India won her independence. Further east the same process went ahead, and in 1949 China's great victory shook the world anew. The outcome of the struggle to end colonialism in Asia was now certain and by 1955, at the time of the Bandung Conference, it could be said that Asia had won a decisive victory over the forces of direct colonial rule. The same process also swept over Africa and the Middle East, so that within a mere five years after Bandung most of Africa had ended direct colonial rule and no one now doubts that, despite the difficult battles which lie ahead, the days of colonial rule in Africa are numbered. Within the next five years the battle will be won.

Why was it possible for the people of Africa to win these battles in the 1960s? Why was it not possible in the 1930s? The explanation lies in the whole character of our epoch, an epoch which is sharply distinguished from all preceding ones.

As a result of the defeat of fascism and the experiences in the second world war, opportunities arose, first in Eastern Europe, and then in Asia, for the people's forces to carry forward their victory over fascism and reaction into a victory for socialism. A mighty socialist camp arose, stretching from the Baltic to the Pacific, from Berlin to Peking, and embracing close on 1,000 million people, or well over a third of the world's population. This was the decisive new factor which was to make possible new advances of the colonial people, and which was to change the character of our epoch. This epoch has now been characterised in the following terms:

"Our time, whose main content is the transition from capitalism to socialism initiated by the Great October Revolution, is a time of struggle between the two opposing social systems, a time of socialist revolutions and national liberation revolutions, a time of the breakdown of imperialism, of the abolition of the colonial system, a time of transition of more peoples to the socialist path, of the triumph of socialism and communism on a world-wide scale.

It is the principle characteristic of our time that the world socialist system is becoming the decisive factor in the development of society. . . . Today it is the world socialist system and the forces fighting against imperialism, for a socialist transformation of society, that determine the main content, main trend and main features of the historical development of society."

(*Statement of the 81 Communist and Workers' Parties, November 1960.*)

In this epoch, into which we have now entered, it is the laws of socialism which will increasingly determine the course of world history. All great popular movements, whether for peace, against fascism, against monopoly or for national independence, are swept into the orbit of the great turnover of the world to socialism, and in the process undergo changes and modifications in their initial character. Movements for national independence today can no longer be confined within the limits of normal bourgeois democracy as in the nineteenth century, for these are anti-imperialist movements taking place at a time of mounting socialist ascendancy in the world. For this reason the national independence movements in Africa, Asia and Latin America, and the new states which they throw up, will increasingly turn in a socialist direction.

Thus, factors in Africa, as well as those in the world situation, offer the most favourable opportunities for the new African states to take a non-capitalist path of development away from colonialism and in the direction of socialism. But favourable factors, by themselves, will not bring about the necessary change. For this to take place the people of Africa will have to take decisive steps to safeguard their national independence, defend their newly won sovereignty, uproot the remaining footholds of imperialism —economic, political, military and ideological—and carry through a sweeping economic, social, political and cultural transformation of their countries which, through radical land reform, industrialisation and the nationalisation of foreign enterprises, will lay the basis for a new life for the people. Such a transformation, making possible the emergence of an independent national democracy, can be fully carried out only if there is the utmost democratic participation by the people themselves in effecting such a change.

The creation of independent national democracies in Africa will not yet mean the establishment of socialist states, nor even the certainty of a direct and relatively rapid change-over to socialism. As their name implies, such states will carry through the completion of all the tasks of the national democratic revolution. They will strive to push the national development to its fullest, and to complete the liberation of the nation in every respect. The ousting of imperialism in all spheres, the carrying through of land reform, industrialisation, the expansion of democracy—these do not yet introduce socialism. For such states to make the transition to socialism there must be a fundamental change within the state and government. Whether these states pass on to socialism or not depends on which class leads the nation. If the national bourgeoisie retains the leadership of the state and nation, then further development will be in a capitalist direction and a struggle to defeat the bourgeoisie will be necessary before the march towards socialism can proceed. If, on the other hand, the working class emerges as the leadership of the independent national democracy, then the transition to socialism will be all the quicker and less painful. Either way, all the countries of Africa will inevitably become socialist; the only question is whether they will allow the developing African bourgeoisie to drag them first towards capitalism, or whether under working-class leadership they take the easier and more direct path.

How the necessary changes can be made, what is involved in making them, what is the character and policy of the forces opposing such changes and what can be learnt from the short experiences of Africa's new states is the subject of the following chapters in this book.

CHAPTER TWO

NEO-COLONIALISM—THE MAIN DANGER

Though most peoples in Africa now possess their own national governments and national flags, their struggle for full independence is by no means over. A hundred and one economic and financial links still bind them to imperialist economy; and the political, military and ideological influence of imperialism still makes itself felt. In short, colonialism is going down to defeat, but neo-colonialism is taking its place.

It is significant that the Third All-African Peoples Conference, meeting at Cairo in March 1961, and reviewing the progress made by the African independence movements in the previous period, came to the conclusion that a new danger threatened Africa—neo-colonialism. It therefore adopted a special resolution on this subject, together with one on the "Liquidation of the Remnants of Imperialism". These resolutions do not confine themselves to generalities, but spell out, in considerable detail, the forms and manifestations of neo-colonialism and of its agents, and the steps which must be taken to defeat it and to uproot the last vestiges of the old order. Moreover, they list the countries from which the neo-colonialist danger comes—United States, Federal Germany, Israel, Britain, Belgium, Holland, South Africa, France.

In discussions on neo-colonialism the impression is sometimes given that it is simply a means of imperialism retaining and extending its economic influence after it has had to surrender its political power. This, of course, is an essential component of neo-colonialism, but the Cairo conference resolution helps us to understand that the phenomenon is far more complex than that, far more all-embracing, and includes every main aspect of life and society through which imperialism can find ways to operate and exert its pressure. The resolution points out that "neo-colonialism, which is the survival of the colonial system in spite of formal recognition of political independence in emerging countries which become the victims of an indirect and subtle form of domination by political, economic, social, military or technical means, is the greatest threat to African countries that have newly won their independence or those approaching this status".

Why "Neo-Colonialism"?

Before analysing in more detail the forms and methods of neo-colonialism, especially in their application to present-day Africa, it is necessary to consider why this phenomenon has arisen, what is there "new" about this form of colonialism as compared with the "old" and whether imperialism has abandoned the "old" form.

In 1919 the total population of the world was 1,777 million, of which 1,230 million, or almost 70 per cent, were in colonies, semi-colonies or dominions. By 1961, out of a total world population of 3,017 million only about 60 million, or 2 per cent, remained in subordinate status. Truly the world has been turned upside down.

Why has this amazing change taken place? Why has such rapid advance been possible? Supporters of western imperialism argue that it was due to western influence, that the concepts of democracy and national independence are themselves "western ideas" which colonial rule had spread in Africa, and that the post-war emergence of independent African states is a logical outcome of western rule. They even argue that they "prepared" Africa for independence and when the time was ripe gracefully withdrew from the scene. To an African, of course, such claims are ridiculous, but they may still have some currency in the West; though even here such beliefs must be wearing thin after seeing how desperately the Belgians tried to hold on to the Congo, how strenuously the French imperialists fought to hold on to Algeria, how stubbornly the British still hold on to most of their possessions in central, eastern and southern Africa, and how ferociously the Portuguese hold on to Angola, Mozambique and their other colonies in Africa. In view of the extravagant claims for British "generosity", made by Tory, Liberal and Labour spokesmen, it is not out of order to point out that while Britain has been compelled to make retreats in Ghana, Nigeria, Sierra Leone and Tanganyika, she still[1] rules Gambia, Kenya, Zanzibar, Nyasaland, Northern Rhodesia, Southern Rhodesia, Bechuanaland, Basutoland, Swaziland and is a key influence in South West Africa and South Africa. Clearly British imperialism is not in any very great hurry to slough off her "imperial responsibilities"; in fact, she retreats only when the peoples compel her to do so.

Since the Treaty of Berlin in 1885—when the big western powers decided to carve up Africa amongst themselves—the people of Africa have conducted a long and many-sided battle for independence. Not a single year has gone by without some action by them. Every year since 1885, now in one territory, now in another, there has been some activity—a strike, a demonstration, a protest movement, the launching of a national paper, the formation of a political organisation, the founding of a trade union, a soldiers' mutiny, the setting up of an independent African school, a boycott, an armed revolt by a whole people—till in the end the movement of the people has become a flood of anti-colonial and anti-imperialist struggle which is sweeping colonialism away from one end of the African continent to the other.

This phenomenon, which is taking place not only in Africa but also in Asia and Latin America, and which is shaking to their very roots not only British imperialism but the imperialist states of France, Belgium, Portugal, Spain, the Netherlands and the United States, shows quite clearly that what is happening cannot be dismissed as the consequences of "British generosity", but that a most profound and powerful historic process is at work. This process is the ending of colonialism.

That the former subject peoples should have won such great victories in the past fifteen years is due to two factors. On the one hand, the people's movements in all colonial countries and those emerging from colonialism have grown into powerful storms

[1] At the moment of writing—December 1962.

which are sweeping the imperialist army into forced retreat. And, secondly, the establishment of a powerful socialist system embracing 1,000 million people, two-fifths of mankind, has weakened imperialism beyond repair. This epoch, which is witnessing the rise of socialism and the downfall of capitalism, is also the epoch of the death of colonialism. And this is a truth which is being increasingly understood by the liberated peoples themselves.

As for the imperialists, they fully understand. That is why they work night and day to prevent the colonial and former colonial peoples establishing close and friendly relations with the Soviet Union and other socialist countries; and this aim on the part of the imperialists represents a key purpose in their policy of neo-colonialism.

This new colonial policy is not a matter of choice. It is history which has driven the imperialists to adopt the mantle of neo-colonialism. As long as it suited their purpose, and as long as their relative strength enabled them to do so, the imperialists ruled Africa, and other territories, by direct arbitrary government and by naked force. Colonialism, the direct and overall subordination—political, economic, military and cultural—of one country by another, on the basis of state power being in the hands of the dominating foreign power, is preferred by imperialism, for it alone, explained Lenin, "gives complete guarantees of success to the monopolies against all the risks of the struggle with competitors . . ." since "in the colonial market it is easier to eliminate competition, to make sure of orders, to strengthen the necessary 'connections', etc., by monopolist methods (and sometimes it is the only possible way)". (V. I. Lenin: *Imperialism—the Highest Stage of Capitalism:* Lawrence & Wishart, 1948 edition, pp. 100–3.)

Further, direct colonial rule gives the imperialist power virtually unfettered control over land, resources and labour, and thus makes possible the utmost exploitation of the people. And, in addition, colonial rule allows the maintenance of military bases which can be used to further imperialist strategies.

Over most of the globe, colonialism can no longer be maintained. The peoples of the world—and not only in the colonial territories—are demanding an end to the infamous system. Voicing these demands, and acting on the initiative of the Soviet government, the United Nations has adopted a resolution calling for the ending of colonialism—a resolution which even most of the imperialist powers found it opportune not to oppose.

In the face of these pressures the imperialists are resorting to different methods in order to retain the essence of their former colonial rule. It is these methods to which the name "neo-colonialism" has been given.

Earlier Forms of Indirect Control

In a sense, neo-colonialism is not an entirely new form. For years indirect forms of rule were practised in China by all the imperialist powers. Outwardly China was independent. She had her own government complete with Chinese ministers, her own national flag and other national institutions, her own diplomatic relations with other powers, and went through all the formal motions of an independent, sovereign power. Constitutionally speaking, the China of Chiang Kai-shek was independent; but in reality she was a victim of colonialism or, as she was sometimes described in those days, a semi-colony. One had only to visit the old China to see the realities of foreign rule: not simply the insulting and humiliating way in which westerners acted in China (the notorious "Dogs and Chinese not admitted" sign at the Shanghai racecourse being only a symbol of such behaviour), but the reserved "International Settlements" in major ports, the western-owned factories and banks, the numerous American, British, German, French and other advisers in government departments, in the armed forces, the police and in other institutions, the western-run newspapers and cinemas—and, above all, the western gunboats lying menacingly in the river outside Shanghai, ever-present reminders of the realities of power.

But China was not the only country where such methods were practised. For years Britain exercised her power in the Middle East without, in the main, the use of direct colonial rule. Iran, Iraq, Egypt and other territories were part of the "British sphere"—but, nominally speaking, these countries enjoyed independent status, just as Jordan does to this very day. But behind King Fuad and King Feisal stood Britain, just as it stands today behind King Hussein, and just as the United States stands behind the Shah of Iran.

Thus, for Britain, the method of ruling without being too obviously seen is a well-tried and tested one. For the United States, too, this is nothing new. For decades United States imperialism has pulled the strings in Liberia, determined its policies and controlled its economy; the entire constitutional system in Liberia is a carbon-copy of the American one. Even Liberia's currency is based on the American dollar. The Philippines, too, has for years been a disguised colonial victim of the United States.

But it is above all in Latin America that U.S. imperialism fashioned and practised this tactic. Mexicans apparently ruled Mexico, Brazilians Brazil, Bolivians Bolivia and Argentinians Argentina. Porfirio Diaz, hated dictator of Mexico, was a Mexican. Vincente Gomez, butcher of Venezuela, was a Venezuelan, as was Jimenez who followed him. The bloody tyrant Trujillo was a son of San Domingo, and Batista, Cuba's sorrow, was Cuban-born. And it was the same in all twenty Latin American republics. Outwardly they were independent—and the rulers of Wall Street and the White House could proclaim unctuously: "We have no colonies. We are not an imperialist power." Just as today they sing the same refrain in an attempt to ensnare the people of Africa and other continents into accepting their approaches as offers from an alleged disinterested friend.

Yet there never was a bigger lie than the myth of America's "anti-colonialism". For the real facts are that in Latin America the United States established one of the cruellest and most bloody—and for Wall Street the most profitable—empires the world has ever seen. A total of $9,000 million—a third of all its foreign investments—has been invested by the U.S. in Latin America. But, according to the U.N. Economic Commission for Latin America, the U.S. monopolies in the period 1946–56 received $3·17 for every dollar invested there, and shipped out of Latin America in the same period profits amounting to $5,600 million. Estimates covering the more recent period show that over the past fifteen years the influx of new capital into Latin America has been $6,500 million, but the profits pumped out have totalled $10,000 million.

But the United States has not only taken profits from the countries of Latin America, not only directed and distorted their economies, condemned them to become dependent on a single commodity—Colombia on coffee, Bolivia on tin, Chile on copper, Honduras on bananas, Venezuela on oil, and Cuba, until recently, on sugar—and restricted their growing of essential foodstuffs and stifled their industrial development. In effect she has ruled most of these countries—and still does. U.S. Ambassadors act as all-powerful monarchs, giving their "advice" to nominally independent governments. At the United Nations the Latin American representatives are given their voting instructions, sometimes quite blatantly. It is said in Latin America that at the Punta del Este Conference in 1962 there was a moment of embarrassment when one Latin American delegate began to read out a speech which had already been read out previously by a delegate from another country; it appeared that the Central Intelligence Agency (C.I.A.) had mixed up the briefs it was handing out.

Militarily, too, the United States has used Latin America as its colonial hinterland, establishing bases, installing its military advisers and imposing "military aid" programmes and agreements.

When American politicians and business men talk about giving "aid" to Africa what they have in mind is the pattern of relations they have established in Latin America, a pattern which provides Wall Street with the profits and Washington with the realities of power, while the people of Latin American countries suffer in poverty and their governments possess only the formal shell of authority and independence.

A New Phase

Thus, in essence, disguised methods of colonialism are not an entirely new form of colonial domination. But yet there is something new in the present situation. This is shown by the fact that between 1945 and 1960 some 1,500 million people liberated themselves from direct colonial rule and established their own indigenous governments. In other words, although indirect colonialism was practised before 1945 it was not yet the dominant characteristic in the underdeveloped regions of the world, certainly not in Africa and only partially in Asia. Today, however, so headlong has been the retreat of direct colonial rule that it can be said that *neo-colonialism has now become the normal pattern, and no longer the exception.* The term, in fact, describes a new phase, the phase after the disintegration of the colonial system, when imperialism tries desperately to seek new footholds for its power. Furthermore, on the basis of previous experience, neo-colonialism has become a far more polished and all-round weapon of imperialism; new refinements have been added, new subtleties and agencies pressed into service.

It should, perhaps, be emphasised that in speaking about the neo-colonialist activities of the imperialist powers, whether in Africa or in other continents, one is not necessarily making a judgment of the government of a newly independent country nor defining its status. Imperialism tries its neo-colonialist tricks everywhere—and sometimes has to be content with only a partial success. Governments and states which are sincerely and bravely fighting their way forward to overcome the vestiges of colonialism often find colonialist footholds still on their soil— and sometimes have, perforce, to put up with them until a more suitable opportunity arises. No one in his right senses would regard Cuba as a neo-colonialist outpost of the United States— yet Cuba, for the moment, has been compelled to allow the U.S. military base to remain on Cuban soil. The Guinea Government is clearly no one's puppet—yet the big international grouping of monopolies, F.R.I.A., still retains its grip on the valuable bauxite processing and another big international grouping, Consafrique, is to undertake the exploitation of the valuable iron ore in Mount Nimba and Mount Simandou. Similarly, French imperialism undoubtedly is trying to make use of Mali's relations with the European Common Market to re-establish France's stranglehold on Mali.

If neo-colonialism is an expression of the weakening of world imperialism, it is also, in a sense, a reflection of the strength or weakness of the anti-imperialist forces. The fact that imperialism has had to turn to neo-colonialism is a sign of its weakness; but the fact that imperialism is able to use forms of neo-colonialism is a sign of the insufficient strength and maturity of the anti-imperialist movements. Where the working class was in the lead of the anti-imperialist movement, as in China, North Korea, North Vietnam and Cuba, the winning of national liberation blocked the entry of neo-colonialism and so made possible a rapid transition to the socialist phase of the revolution. Where the national movements are united and the working class plays a key but not yet decisive role in the new states, as in Ghana, Guinea or Mali, neo-colonialism finds the going heavy. But where the national movements are divided, where feudal and reactionary capitalist forces are at the head of the new states, and where the working class is under attack (as in most of the French-speaking states) or seriously divided and insufficiently developed (as in Nigeria or Sierra Leone), neo-colonialism almost enjoys a field-day.

There is one other warning that should be made in assessing the results of neo-colonialist activity. All the new African states and governments are in a process of transition; they are under the constant pressure of their own peoples, who are not content to sit still or slumber amid the ruins of collapsed colonialism; and they are influenced, too, by the new world situation, by the world-wide storm of anti-imperialist sentiment and by the growing, powerful socialist camp whose laws of development are increasingly stamping their imprint on the march of all mankind.

For this reason, the new government whose leaders yesterday seemed too timid in the face of imperialism, and who had not yet learnt to straighten their backs in the face of big business and its military backers, may today stand up, demand the removal of military bases, and take over, into national hands, the enterprises formerly in the grasp of foreign monopolies. The last fifteen years is replete with examples of such metamorphoses and it would be foolish to expect that further changes are not in store.

Perhaps nothing illustrates this fact better than the changes to be observed in a number of the French states formerly under French colonial rule and which are generally regarded as being, to some extent, in France's pocket. The President of the Upper Volta, for instance, has demanded the withdrawal of French troops. Senegal has opened up diplomatic and economic relations with the Soviet Union and other socialist countries. So has Dahomey, whose Vice-President, Sourou-Migan Apithy, during the negotiations in Moscow, made a statement which clearly went a long way beyond the formal politeness sometimes associated with such occasions. Vice-President Apithy admitted that before coming to the Soviet Union "we had certain misgivings and this was understandable when one thinks of the bitter campaign of discrimination and lies which is conducted against the Soviet Union". But his visit helped him to see things as they really are and to come to the conclusion that the Soviet Union "has advanced to the vanguard of progress, thanks to the efforts of its working people and the wisdom of its leaders, and also thanks to Marxism-Leninism". He ended by saying that the cruiser *Aurora*, which gave the signal for the 1917 revolution, "belongs not to the Soviet Union alone, but to all mankind, to all who suffer, all who languish under the colonial yoke, all who are exploited". (In an interview with the *Moscow News*, 9 June 1962.)

It should not be thought that the turn from normal colonialism to neo-colonialism is absolute. The imperialists are just as ready, in certain cases, to maintain direct rule and to back it up with open force; the only question for them is: Can they still do this? And does the situation demand it? As already mentioned above, Britain still rules directly over most of its territories in Africa, and is clearly in no haste to abandon the benefits of direct rule. France tried for over seven years to subdue Algeria by force of arms—and finally ceased this attempt only when it became clear that the Algerian people could not be conquered. Belgium and the United States have shown in the Congo that even the granting of formal independence does not rule out the use of force by imperialism in order to ensure capitulation by the new state.

Spain still holds on to its possessions in the north and the west, and has shown itself prepared to use force in order to maintain its hold. Portugal, too, favours direct rule and the use of violent repression to maintain a full colonial system, as do the rulers of South Africa.

But, all the same, the world moves. These desperate attempts by Portugal and Spain, the bitter war in Algeria, the holocaust in the Congo, Britain's reluctance to give way in Central Africa or in Kenya, and Verwoerd's desperate arms build-up in South Africa, are the last, dying kicks of the mortally wounded beast. Death is sweeping over colonialism and its final gasp cannot be long delayed.

"Nothing Can Stop This"

It is precisely in answer to this new situation that the imperialist powers are calling up the reserves of neo-colonialism. Nothing illustrates the dilemma of the imperialists better than the utterances of some of the leading bourgeois statesmen.

Thus de Gaulle, already a year before the cease-fire agreement with Algerian F.L.N., was pleading with his army officers to understand that the world had changed, that, in the words of the popular song, "fings ain't wot they used t'be", that the old method of ruling Algeria solely by force of arms could not be maintained, and that it was, after all, not a matter of choice (one can note in his speech only too well how much de Gaulle regrets this) but a question of facing the facts of life.

"The work of France in Algeria must go on, and it is only too evident that it cannot go on under the conditions of yesterday. One may regret this, and you will realize that a man of my age and background may have his regrets at that which probably could have been done earlier and which was left undone. . . .

But when one assumes national responsibilities one must take the problem as a whole, as it is—and such as it is, it cannot be dealt with as in days gone by. . . .

From the fact of insurrection itself, the population of this Algeria . . . has acquired an awareness which it did not previously have. Nothing can stop this. It is also true that the insurrection, and all that is connected with it, is taking place in a new world, in a world which is not at all like the world I knew myself when I was young. There is—you are all aware of this—the whole context of emancipation which is sweeping the world from one end to another, which has swept over our Black Africa, which has swept, without exception, over all those which once were empires, and which cannot but have considerable consequences here. . . ."

(Extracts from a speech by General de Gaulle to French officers at Blida, 9 December 1960.)

The same recognition of the realities of the situation is to be found in Macmillan's famous "wind of change" speech which he made in Cape Town on 3 February 1960.

"The most striking of all the impressions I have formed since I left London a month ago, is of the strength of this African national consciousness.... The wind of change is blowing through the continent.

Whether we like it or not, this growth of national consciousness is a political fact. We must accept it as a fact. Our national policies must take account of it...."

In the speeches of Macmillan and de Gaulle, as well as in a number of policy documents and statements of British politicians and government departments, one can sense the dilemma of imperialism. Neither de Gaulle nor Macmillan greets the growth of African national consciousness with open arms; neither of them congratulates the African people on having struggled so strenuously for independence and against colonialism. On the contrary, for both it is a regretful recognition of the facts of life. The world has changed, imperialism is weaker, socialism is stronger, and the peoples of Africa, Asia and Latin America are determined to be free. For imperialism the question has become: How to readapt itself to this new situation?

The British ruling class is the oldest and most experienced ruling class in the world. For centuries it has learnt how to live through periods of storm. When trade unions were first formed in Britain the ruling class tried to crush them out of existence. Despite repression, however, the workers continued to organise, and the capitalists were at last compelled to retreat. But it was not a complete retreat. Having been compelled to accept the existence of trade unions, the capitalists then devoted their efforts to preventing the trade unions becoming a too serious and direct danger to themselves. They worked to smother the healthy, militant working-class ideas of the trade unionists, and they bent their efforts to winning over trade union leaders. Their motto was: "If you can't beat 'em, join 'em." And when one contemplates the stolid, satisfied faces of today's trade union peers, and notes the unwillingness of the T.U.C. General Council to make any fundamental challenge to the British capitalist class, it would be difficult to pretend that the British rulers have not had a substantial measure of success.

In a sense the British rulers are following the same policy in Africa. Seeing they can no longer crush the national movements out of existence, they are now turning to the aim of trying to influence these movements, to keep the new states "with the

West"—which means maintaining them in the orbit of imperialism—and so prevent them from gaining complete independence.

The ways in which this is done are manifold. But it is important
to see them in their entirety because it helps one to understand
the various mechanisms employed by neo-colonialism and to see
how this new total system operates. It should, perhaps, be said
at the outset that the tactic of neo-colonialism is not one of
alliance of imperialism with the entire national movement—
an impossible task, for the masses who back the movement are
not to be so easily fooled or satisfied—but an agreement with an
upper section of the national movement at the expense of the
full economic, social and political development of the newly
independent states, and thus at the expense of the workers and
peasants who are the majority of the population in these states.

All neo-colonialist activities of British imperialism in Africa
must be examined in relation to this central strategic aim.

Redeployment of Imperialist Cadres

Perhaps the first thing which should be emphasised is that
although neo-colonialism involves the making of political concessions by the colony-owning powers, it does not, in any sense,
mean the abandonment by these powers of their political aims
towards the former colonies, nor the sudden complete withdrawal
of imperialist personnel who can safeguard imperial interests.
For a start, even after a British colony wins independence, it is
usually the case that a British Governor-General is installed—
and sometimes, as in the case of Sierra Leone, he is, at first,
simply the former Governor. Theoretically the Governor-
General's power is only nominal, but in practice he is able to
wield considerable influence. In Nigeria the depth of national
feeling compelled the replacement of the British Governor-
General by Dr. Azikiwe—but at the same time the Nigerian
Federal Prime Minister, Sir Abubakar Balewa, retained a
British official, Mr. Peter Stallard, as his Private Secretary, until
widespread protests in Nigeria compelled the British Government
to remove Stallard (it sent him out to be Governor in British
Honduras).

Other British officials and civil servants remain, very often in key positions, throughout the state apparatus of the newly independent states—although the struggle for the "Africanisation of the civil service", which is waged in all African countries, compels the British Government to make retreats on this front, step by step. How necessary the struggle against these "delayed-action bombs" really is has been conveyed by President Nkrumah in his autobiography, in which he describes very frankly the sabotage his government faced from the British civil servants in its early days:

". . . it did not escape my notice that where the administrative service was concerned, if a policy was laid down for the officials by the Government with which they disagreed, means were adopted, by subterfuge or otherwise, to wreck that policy. At other times I would find that matters that I wanted to be dealt with urgently would be delayed indefinitely (because they were not approved of by some of the officials) until I had to intervene and get the job done. . . . It happened too often for it to be a coincidence that whenever Government policy was to be put into effect, the officials either dilly-dallied or saw that nothing was done about it. Again, I could at one time almost guarantee that if there was any movement afoot against the Government, every attempt was made on the part of the civil service to enhance the opposition against the Government."

(*Ghana: the Autobiography of Kwame Nkrumah:* 1959 edition, p.125.)

President Nkrumah draws the valuable lesson:

". . . after any political revolution, non-violent or violent, the new government should, immediately on coming to power, clear out from the civil service all its old leaders. My own experience taught me that by failing to do so, a revolutionary government risks its own destruction."

(ibid., p. 122.)

In Tanganyika, too, voices were raised immediately after independence, insisting on the rapid promotion of Africans to key positions in the state. Up to that time, Sir Ernest Vasey, a former colonial official in Kenya, had been Minister of Finance in the interim government—but the widespread feeling in favour of national cadres compelled his resignation.

One department of state in which British officials continue to play a key role for some time is in the key sectors of the armed forces and the police. It is significant, in this respect, that when President Nkrumah faced a temporary crisis in the autumn of 1961 he found it necessary to dismiss General Alexander from his position as Chief of Staff of Armed Forces in order to be certain of the security of the state. Similarly, the Tanganyika Government in April 1962 found it necessary to replace their British chief of police by an African. In other spheres of government, in economic departments and different sections of the state apparatus, the British Government endeavours to leave behind its trained personnel in order to safeguard its former interests.

In addition to the use of British political personnel who are left behind at the time of granting political independence, British imperialism makes the utmost use of additional forces which are being sent to the newly independent countries. In fact, to step up the number of British cadres who can be sent out to former colonial territories, the British Government has now established a special department—the Department of Technical Co-operation, headed by Sir Andrew Cohen, who formerly served British imperialism in several posts, as head of the African Department of the Colonial Office, as Governor of Uganda and as British representative on the Trusteeship Council at the United Nations. The new department was started off with the considerable staff of 1,000 and a financial allocation of £30 million. Its responsibilities include "technical training in the United Kingdom and Overseas, the provision of experts, administrators and other professional men and women, and the supply of advisory, technical and consultant services". (Statement in the House of Commons, 25 April 1961.)

In commenting on the setting up of the new department and the proposed appointment of Sir Andrew Cohen, with the simultaneous appointment of Sir Hugh Foot as Britain's spokesman on the U.N. Trusteeship Council, *The Times* (24 April 1961) comments:

"*The colonial empire may shrink and the Commonwealth may change its form, but Britain's overseas responsibilities to the underdeveloped countries go on, changed but undiminished. These changes mean re-deployment of manpower, not only at the bottom and in the middle ranges but at the top. And if Britain is to hold her place in the world, this redeployment is a matter for the exercise of the highest skill in fitting the man for the job.*"

And *The Times* then comments that "No two men have played a greater part" (than Sir Andrew Cohen and Sir Hugh Foot) "in their two ways in turning a now outdated colonial empire into an association of free peoples." Sir Andrew Cohen's views on Africa's future relations with British imperialism were adequately expressed in his book *Changing Africa,* in which he warned that "In the African countries . . . nationalist movements are bound to grow steadily more powerful" and that in consequence "the intelligent thing" for the British Government was "to recognise this early, and by skilful anticipation to try and guide the energies of nationalists into constructive channels." As for Sir Hugh Foot, his reputation largely rests on his ability to rescue British imperialism from its difficulties in Cyprus and to carry through a settlement which, while giving Cyprus certain sovereign rights, safeguarded for Britain her investments and, more important still, her military interests and nuclear bases.

Thus, when *The Times* refers to the key role played by these two men "in turning a now outdated colonial empire into an association of free peoples" it is simply stressing that Sir Andrew and Sir Hugh have played a key role in fashioning British imperialism's neo-colonialist tactics in the post-war period. The new Department of Technical Co-operation is a major weapon for the carrying through of this new policy.

Because military power and influence plays such a key role it is understandable that once direct military domination of a country has ceased imperialism should be concerned to find new ways of retaining military influence. Where possible, military bases are retained and even new ones established, sometimes in the teeth of bitter local opposition. Both Nigeria and Sierra Leone were compelled to reach military understandings with Britain as the price for political independence; and though, in the former case, the protests of the Nigerian people compelled a formal withdrawal of the agreement, the very wording of this withdrawal shows that in reality Britain's military interests in

Nigeria have been preserved. In countries which have still to gain their political independence, such as Kenya and Zanzibar, the question of ending foreign bases is a major point in the current demands of the national movements.

Apart from military bases, British imperialism also tries to safeguard its former military influence by retaining, where possible, its monopoly in the supply of arms and, as a natural corollary, the training of local forces in the use of such arms. The retention of British officers in the armed forces of newly independent countries is normal practice; even in Ghana key military positions were held by British officers until late 1961; and today, still, through training arrangements and the provision of military advisers and technicians, Britain wields considerable military influence in the new African states. The British Government is also very eager to train African officers in British military, naval and air-force academies. This is not done on a large scale, but is sufficient to give rise to the hope on the part of the British authorities that they will be able to establish connections and build up influence with tomorrow's leading military figures in the new states. With the experience of anti-democratic military coups in Sudan and Pakistan, and attempts in Ceylon and elsewhere, the possible dangers that may arise from independent countries having their officers trained by the former occupying power are obvious.

The retention of military influence in the former French-occupied territories of Africa is even more marked than in those under former British control. French troops, bases, military commanders and military agreements are the usual pattern everywhere, except in Guinea and Mali. It is noticeable that African troops from some of the former French territories were even utilised in Algeria, fighting against the F.L.N.; and France's testing of nuclear weapons in the Sahara has gone virtually unchallenged by most of the former French colonies in Africa.

Ideological Weapons

Along with efforts to influence the new states through the use of personnel from the metropolitan country and by various military means, the imperialists are paying special attention to questions of propaganda and ideology. As far as the former British colonies in Africa are concerned, there has been a big move in the last few years by major British newspaper proprietors to take over a substantial section of the African press. The *Daily Mirror* group under Mr. Cecil King, for example, acquired the *Sunday Mirror* and *Daily Graphic* in Ghana, the *Daily Times* and *Sunday Times* in Nigeria, and the *Daily Mail* in Freetown. Similarly, the powerful Thomson group owns the *Daily Express*, the *Sunday Express* and the weekly magazine *The Service*, in Nigeria, and has recently established links with East African Newspapers Ltd., which publishes and distributes fourteen different newspapers and magazines in Kenya, Tanganyika, Uganda and Zanzibar.

Thomson's has also acquired controlling interests over the Salisbury *Daily News* and thirteen weekly, fortnightly and monthly publications in the Central African Federation, as well as control of the *Nyasaland Times* and most other publications in Nyasaland. His group has also bought seven publications in Southern Rhodesia and twenty-two in the Republic of South Africa.

In the field of radio, too, apart from direct B.B.C. broadcasts to Africa, and certain indirect B.B.C. influences, commercial companies are also looking for openings. In Kenya, for example, a private T.V. company has been established, with the assistance of the Thomson group. Thus, in countries now winning independence, or which have recently won it, British imperialism has created additional propaganda weapons with which to influence public opinion, spread misunderstanding and rumour and inculcate outlooks and attitudes harmful to national growth in these countries.

These efforts are being supplemented by the opening up of "Information Centres" and suchlike. The British Council, for example, has opened three new such centres in French-speaking Africa; the British Foreign Office is opening new posts in Dakar, Leopoldville, Abidjan and Brazzaville; the Colonial Office has established a new centre in Zanzibar; and the Commonwealth Relations Office one in Sierra Leone.

In 1962 the new Department of Technical Co-operation, which is as we have seen an important neo-colonialist institution, spent nearly £22 million on "overseas information services".

With all these important means of propaganda at their disposal, or at least open to their influence, the British imperialists are concentrating on spreading certain conceptions not only amongst leading circles they aim to win over, but also amongst the broad mass of people whom they hope to confuse.

During the events in Ghana in the early autumn of 1961, when a number of anti-government activities were organised by imperialism in collaboration with local reactionary forces, the British-owned press gave encouragement to the Opposition. This so angered the Ghanaian workers that a subsequent regional conference of the Ghana Trades Union Congress demanded the "immediate nationalisation of the foreign press" as it was "a mouthpiece of imperialist agents". Eventually, in July 1962, the Ghana Government took steps to acquire financial control over the Cecil King papers in Ghana by ordering that the shares of the Ghana Graphic Company Limited be bought by a board of trustees appointed by the Ghana Government.

In waging its ideological warfare, imperialism uses a variety of slogans and arguments to mislead African opinion. It encourages corruption and ideas of personal careerism, and fosters all the worst, most commercialised and degraded aspects of the "Western way of life"; it preaches "non-violence" and passive acceptance of suffering on the one hand, but personal dictatorship and tribal violence on the other; it presses every divisive and disruptive demand into service, and strives to turn Africa back to the obscurantism and narrow horizons of the past.

Above all, it beats on the drum of anti-communism. This, above all, is the secret weapon of neo-colonialism. Its aim is to isolate the African people from the powerful socialist camp which can render such valuable material assistance to the new states; to quarantine Africa from the liberating ideas of scientific socialism, of Marxism-Leninism; and to disrupt the African national movements by turning the more moderate sections against the most militant. It is a measure of the danger, and partial success of these tactics, that some African national figures, when labelled "communist" by imperialism, tend to regard the charge as an insult, instead of treating it with the contempt it deserves. In other words, the imperialist allegation that "communism is bad" is essentially accepted by such people. As long as people are scared of the term "communist", the neo-colonialists will have a weapon with which to disrupt the national movements.

Economic Aims

There is, of course, no space here to deal in detail with all the various forms and manifestations of neo-colonialism. Many of them are listed and explained in the Resolution on Neo-Colonialism passed by the Third All-African Peoples Congress. But vital to the aims of imperialism are the economic aspects of neo-colonialism. Economic interest is a dominant goal of neo-colonialism; and economic policy is, perhaps, the most important weapon in the entire neo-colonialist arsenal.

In brief one can say that Britain's economic activities in her former colonial possessions in Africa (as well as in her still existing possessions in east, central and southern Africa) have more than one aim. They are directed towards safeguarding present British investments and economic assets; facilitating further British investments and trade; fighting off the "encroachments" of other imperialist powers, especially the United States and Western Germany; and nurturing those class forces in Africa which will tend to be an ally of British imperialism, or at least less resolute opponents of its activities.

In the main Britain still retains her major economic assets in Africa, especially in mining, shipping, banking, insurance, trade and plantations. This is true even in Ghana, although steps have been taken by the Ghana Government to acquire five of the seven main British-owned gold-mining companies, and to buy out British shares in civil aviation, cable and wireless, and other enterprises.

At the same time British monopolies are also making new investments in Africa, not only in traditional fields but also in new manufacturing ventures. Even the United Africa Company is changing from being a purchaser of cash crops into a trader in more specialised lines, such as engineering products, and is entering the general field of manufacture in Africa.

To protect these interests, and at the same time its general political aims, British imperialism has made certain modifications in its economic policy towards the newly independent states— and also in those states which are not yet free from colonial domination. A major component of British neo-colonialism in Africa is the nurturing of class forces which will tend to be allies of British imperialism. In countries such as Ghana, Nigeria or Sierra Leone, where there is no large-scale British settler-population and where, in consequence, a certain local bourgeoisie has grown up, British neo-colonialism aims to work with this new capitalist class, or with sections of it, while not completely abandoning its older feudal allies which it can still use as a threat or at least as a nuisance to the new national governments or the national organisations.

Ideological pressure and economic benefits are both used in order to persuade the African bourgeoisie and petty-bourgeoisie that they have a vested interest in maintaining the British connection, and in following a capitalist path of development in their own country.

To this end, even before the granting of independence, British imperialism offers Africans relatively high scales of salary as Members of Legislative Assemblies, and later as Ministers of Government, as officials in various departments of the State, and so on. The normal figure has been near £1,000 a year as an M.P., and £3,000 a year as Minister. While in Britain the figure is some 50 per cent higher than these amounts, the gap between the average worker in Britain and an M.P. is about two or three to one; whereas in Africa, taking into account average wages of three or four shillings a day, the gap is in the neighbourhood of fifteen or twenty to one. Thus, the danger arises—and this is a precise aim of British imperialism—that African political leaders and M.P.s will, economically speaking, become very quickly isolated from the mass of workers and peasants, will forget their needs and demands, and will tend to regard the maintenance of their economically privileged position as their main aim. The introduction of the capitalist "rat-race" is a major weapon of neo-colonialism.

Such a process does not always take place. And it certainly does not happen overnight. Over a period of years, British policy in Nigeria, for example, gradually made positions open to Africans, utilising this time gained to seek out the most likely allies, to feel its way, to find out and sound out people, and to do things slowly enough to ensure that Britain retained as much initiative as possible. The whole British "theory" of independence in stages is not simply a device for putting off the "evil day". Rather, it is a device for gradually building up a buffer stratum with vested interests, "Western" ways of thought, and amenable to "reason". Above all, Britain tries to avoid the sudden change overnight which might throw the most militant forces to the top. Evolution is not only a theory; it is a quite deliberate tactic of British imperialism. *Gradual change under British guidance is the aim.*

This policy of the British Colonial Office is also being followed by the big companies. British banks, the United Africa Company and other big enterprises in Africa are beginning to make places for a few selected Africans on their managerial staffs, even on their boards of directors. A career in a British-owned firm is thus held out to the new African bourgeoisie and petty-bourgeois forces as an alternative to nationalisation and African control. Even though the numbers involved in all this are relatively small, for each one who finds a privileged post of this kind, whether in politics or private enterprise, there are ten who hope to reach such a position.

In east and central Africa where, owing to substantial white settlement, an African bourgeoisie hardly exists, this same tactic has had to be pursued in a more devious way. In essence, it has become British policy in east and central Africa to create what it officially terms "an African middle class", with whom it hopes to come to terms at the expense of the mass of workers and peasants and at the expense of the progressive development of the new states that are arising in this part of Africa. Report after report, speech after speech, reflects this search for an ally, this need to create an "African middle class". Policies on land, education, trade unions, wages and the franchise are all directed towards the imperialist's neo-colonialist aim of setting up a new prop on which to lean, of driving a wedge into the African national movements, separating the bourgeois and petty-bourgeois forces from the masses, and pushing the former more and more into a position of economic and political dependence on the imperialist powers.

All that has been said above regarding the forms and methods of British neo-colonialism in Africa should be seen within the context of British imperialism's over-all strategy of shifting its former alliance with feudal and tribal chiefs over to one of alliance with the new African bourgeois forces. This new tactic, of course, necessitates a form of influence more indirect than previously, and carries greater dangers. It is, in effect, a less secure method than the old. But since the old method of direct repression, plus an alliance with feudal and tribal chiefs, has broken down, this new method of neo-colonialism is the only course open to imperialism if it wishes to retain its hold.

Neo-colonialism is a method, a tactic, used by other imperialist powers in addition to Britain. Even small capitalist states such as Israel or Sweden, hiding behind the fact that they do not possess colonies, are pressed into service by American and West German imperialism as neo-colonialist agencies which provide technical training services as well as channels for United States and West German investments. As for the United States and West Germany, they make special play with the fact that they are without colonial possessions; but no imperialist powers are more energetic than they in seeking to establish their footholds on the African continent. There is not a single African state where these two powers are not active, investing capital, building trade connections, spreading propaganda, offering scholarships, influencing government policy and seeking for African politicians who can be bought. Kennedy's "Peace Corps", West German "cultural missions", trade union missions from the I.C.F.T.U., jazz-band leaders, missionaries of every denomination—all these and many more, not forgetting the ever-present Mr. Mennen Williams, President Kennedy's special roving ambassador in Africa, are agencies through which the U.S. State Department or the Bonn Government hopes to secure a grip on Africa. Japanese imperialism, too, has shown a new interest in Africa in recent months and is beginning to invest heavily in certain enterprises, and to build up its connections.

Collective Colonialism and Common Market

A specific feature of neo-colonialism is that in addition to being a new method practised by all the imperialist powers it is also a form in which they can *jointly* carry on and even intensify their exploitation of the former colonial peoples. The term "collective colonialism" has been used to describe these new joint efforts. At rock-bottom, this development of collective colonialism is based on the new big financial consortiums being established, especially in Africa, by the big international monopolies. Thus, operating in Gabon is the Iron Ore Company of Mekambo, including French, West German, Italian, Dutch, Belgian and American capital; exploiting the iron ore of Mauretania is a big new corporation, M.I.F.E.R.M.A., with French, British, West German and Italian capital; in Guinea there is F.R.I.A., a big trust with French, American, British and Swiss capital, exploiting the bauxite; West German, French, British and American firms are found acting jointly in big concerns exploiting Saharan oil and gas; and so on, throughout Africa.

Collective colonialism also operates through various international agencies and, as seen in the Congo, can even work via the United Nations. A major form of collective colonialism is the European Common Market, a main aim of which is to assist the big French, and even more the West German, monopolies to step up their exploitation of the sixteen associated African states, and to penetrate the rest of Africa. President Nkrumah has therefore denounced the European Common Market as "an attempt to replace the old system of colonial exploitation by a new system of collective colonialism which will be stronger and more dangerous than the old evils we are striving to liquidate from our continent". (Address to the Conference of African Freedom Fighters, Ghana, 4–6 June 1962.) In fact, the European Common Market is openly based on the conception of "Eurafrica", with Africa providing cheap raw materials for West European industry and importing her relatively high-priced manufactured goods, and at the same time making available a strategic base for imperialism in the event of war.

The experience of the sixteen associated states fully shows how the European Common Market acts as a device to hold back economic development in Africa and keep her people poor. First, despite the claim that the Common Market would provide better prices to these states for their raw materials exports, the gap between the prices of their exports and those of their imports continues to grow. Between 1949 and 1959 the *volume* of exports from the African members of the "Franc Area" went up by 90 per cent, but their export *incomes* by only 10 per cent. (See *Financial Times*, 3 May 1961.) Secondly, association with the Common Market threatens the new, struggling industries of these African states. Formally speaking, the Rome Treaty allows the associated states to put up protective tariffs to safeguard their industries. The only snag is that any measure of this kind has to be sanctioned by the Common Market Commission—which is the European Common Market powers who are busy trying to force their manufactured goods into Africa. This really is setting a thief to catch a thief!

Even the £200 million Development Fund, set up by the European Common Market ostensibly to assist the economic growth of the associated African states, has become an obstacle to such advance. Apart from the fact that the money allocated for sixteen states inhabited by some 50 million people, to be spent over five years, is only sufficient for an amount equivalent to less than a halfpenny a head a day—and apart, also, from the fact that up to August 1961, that is to say after four-fifths of the time had elapsed, only about £40 million, one-fifth of the total, had actually been spent—the use of the fund has in no sense helped forward industrial development. As one London journal has pointed out:

"These sums of money could be utilised rationally only if the Africans could use them at their own discretion. However, they have no right to do so. The Fund authorities spend the money first and foremost in the interests of foreign capital." (*African Trade and Development:* September 1962, p. 13.)

Consequently the bulk of the money allocated from the Development Fund has gone to step up the production of export crops and to improve railways, roads and harbours connected with transporting Africa's mineral wealth away to the metropolitan countries. Proposals put forward by the associated states for the use of the funds for industrial purposes in Africa—for example, the suggestion of the Upper Volta for piping oil and natural gas from the Sahara fields to West Africa—are rejected by the European Common Market fund controllers who prefer to pipe the gas to Europe, even as far as Britain. By 1 January 1962, despite the fact that some two hundred projects had been put forward by the African associated states (and of these, more than half had been rejected outright), work had actually begun on only six, totalling about £600,000, or about 0·3 per cent of the £40 million so far allocated.

The Development Fund clearly provides little aid, if any, to Africa. *The Economist* has cynically remarked of the Fund: "This kind of money is enough to keep the associated states generally

friendly for the present, towards Europe." It may certainly do
that as far as some of the African governments are concerned,
but the African people are beginning to see through all these
new neo-colonialist tricks. Not for nothing did the Third All-
African Peoples Conference in March 1961 call on the African
people to "intensify the struggle against the European Common
Market".

CHAPTER THREE

ECONOMIC ADVANCE AND
ECONOMIC INDEPENDENCE

A common slogan in Africa is "Now we must have economic independence." This idea is natural enough, since a major reason why the people of Africa have taken over the running of their countries is the ambition to lift their homeland out of the category of "economically underdeveloped" regions, to build up their economies and so make it possible to raise their material standards of living and provide adequate social and cultural facilities. To carry out this tremendous task requires a complete transformation of the economy of the African countries—and this involves, in the main, agrarian reform (changes in land tenure, including repossession by the African people of their lands at present in foreign hands, the diversification of agriculture, the promotion of producer co-operatives, and an extension of scientific farming methods), the ending of foreign control of finance and trade, the restoration of all means of production to the African people, and the building of a national industry. Unless the imperialist grip on the economy is broken, no fundamental progress is possible.

If one examines the various African territories, both those still under direct colonial rule and those which have recently won their political independence, one finds that, despite local differences, there is a certain essential similarity in the character of their economies. It is true that independent states such as Ghana, Guinea, Mali, Egypt and others are now making strenuous efforts to overcome their economic backwardness and to change the structure of their economies; but even these countries still carry the heavy burden of their colonial heritage.

Raw Materials Appendages of the West

The pattern has been that African territories have been compelled by imperialist rule and by imperialist economic power to serve as raw materials appendages for western industry and western food consumption. Africa's valuable mineral wealth—gold, diamonds, copper, iron ore, manganese, bauxite, cobalt, uranium, tin, silver, oil and so on—as well as her food and industrial crops (cocoa, coffee, sisal, palm oil, ground nuts, bananas, tobacco, cloves, cotton, etc.), have been shipped to the west, for consumption by western industry and trade. The African territories, as a rule, have had little industry of their own. Usually only the preliminary processing of raw materials has been done on the spot, while the final industrial use of the material has been preserved for the metropolitan countries.

As recently as January 1961 the *Economic Bulletin for Africa* (published by the U.N. Economic and Social Committee) pointed out that "The bulk of African trade is still conducted with present or former metropolitan countries, which means that ... Western Europe continues to dominate the trade of African countries." And this trade is based on Africa exporting cheap raw materials and importing higher-priced manufactured goods.

The western powers have been able to build up this relationship not only because their political domination enabled them, both by legislation and by means of force and pressure, to enforce such a pattern, but also because their ownership of large tracts of the best land, their seizure of key mineral resources, their possession of all the commanding heights of the economy gave them an absolute monopoly over economic policy. Even where the African people were able to develop a sector of their own, as in the field of cash crops, the domination of trade and of the market by the big imperialist monopolies was sufficient to compel the African producers to submit to economic realities and sell their produce accordingly.

Consequently, African countries have been prevented from producing for themselves the manufactured goods which they require, but have been compelled to buy from other sources, usually the western imperialist powers. As a result, Africa has been forced to give up its natural riches to the imperialists at the lowest possible price, but has to pay correspondingly higher prices for the goods the imperialist powers sell to her. Imperialist ownership of trade, shipping, banking and insurance all helps to preserve this unequal relationship.

Unfair Price Relationship

It is not usually recognised how much Africa and other underdeveloped regions are robbed each year by the imperialist countries as a result of the unfair price relationship. A special U.N. study in 1949 showed that between 1897 and 1938 the average prices of primary products fell by approximately a third in relation to those of manufactured goods. A further U.N. study (*Economic Problems*, No. 600, 20 June 1959) points out that the increase in prices of industrial goods and the decline in prices of raw materials represented a loss in import capacity for underdeveloped countries of approximately "the equivalent of six years of loans to underdeveloped countries by the International Bank for Reconstruction and Development, on the basis of 1956–7 prices". The authors of this study estimate the loss suffered by the producer countries through this scissors spread of prices as being more than $2 million. Pierre Moussa (*Les Nations Proletaires:* Paris, 1960, p. 20) calculates that, on the basis that the exports of basic products by the non-industrialised areas of the world amount to about £25 billion, "an adjustment of prices of 14 per cent would therefore suffice to increase the annual income of the *Tiers-Monde* (Third World) by £3·5 billion, the present total of all public aid to under-developed countries". A United Nations Report in 1961 (*International Economic Assistance to the Less Developed Countries*) reveals that between 1953–5 and 1957–9 the loss through the worsening in terms of trade for underdeveloped countries was nearly twice the total amount of public aid funds these countries received.

If the western imperialist powers, which talk so much about "aid" to Africa, were sincere, then there would be no need for loans or investments; all they would need to do would be to give Africa fair prices for her raw materials and charge her less for her manufactured goods. But this is the last thing the imperialist powers are likely to do—unless forced to. To expect them, of their own free will, to remove the unequal price relationship between imperialism and Africa is like expecting them to get off Africa's back. That they will only do when pushed.

In short, African territories have been deliberately held back by imperialism, so as not to be able to compete, and thus have been maintained as a source of "super-profits" for the big western monopolies. Under these conditions, the accumulation of capital in Africa, instead of being directed towards the expansion of African economy, is pumped out of Africa to fill the pockets of dividend holders in New York, London, Paris, Bonn, Brussels, Lisbon and other western centres.

Deprived of this wealth, African agriculture tends to stagnate or deteriorate; neither the impoverished African peasants nor the economically handicapped new African states are able to provide sufficient funds for farm machines, seeds, fertilisers, pest-killing chemicals, or for large-scale irrigation, afforestation, land-clearance or the drainage of swamp lands.

Deprived of this wealth, the new states are also severely handicapped in building up the industries which, in addition to providing the machines, electricity and chemicals for agricultural development, could make possible a constant expansion of production in all fields and provide a continuous source of accumulation both for economic development and for raising the people's standard of living.

Everywhere one travels in Africa, whether in the remaining colonial territories or in the newly independent states, one cannot help being struck by the signs on every hand of the disastrous effects of the colonial system. In building, transport, agriculture, forestry, even frequently in the mines, there is a woeful lack of machinery; the most common "machine" is the human body—hands, feet, shoulders, back and even head being pressed into service to carry goods or work raw materials with the simplest of tools. Extreme poverty, disease, illiteracy and poor housing are the natural consequence of such an economic base.

Such is the outcome of colonial rule—and even in the new African states the heritage of imperialist domination remains the major obstacle to economic advancement; and as long as the imperialist monopolies still hold the commanding heights of economic power (mineral wealth, trade, banks, insurance, shipping, electric power, land and plantations) there is little chance of Africa breaking through the barriers of "underdevelopment". For such a leap forward to take place it is essential, at some stage, for an energetic challenge to be made to these monopolies and for their economic power to be taken away—if not in one fell swoop, then by stages, depending on internal and external circumstances.

The experience already gained by the independent African states, as well as that of the independent states of Asia, shows that, despite certain variations, all these states, in trying to win economic independence and build up their economies, can only make progress by following certain principles which we may call the laws of development of independent states.

These laws include industrialisation, agrarian reform, the creation of a state sector of the economy, economic planning, the nationalisation of foreign enterprises, banking and trade, and the development of economic relations with socialist countries.

Industrialisation—the Key

Key to the destruction of the old colonial pattern is industrialisation. It is no accident that the countries with the highest standards of living in the world, whether capitalist or socialist, are industrialised. It is the main industrialised areas of the world—Europe, North America and Australasia—which enjoy the highest standards; whereas in the non-industrialised, agrarian-mineral regions of Asia, Africa and Latin America average income per head is but a fraction of that in the rest of the world. Even in industralised Europe, it is the areas of least industrial development, such as Portugal, Spain, southern Italy, Sicily or Greece where conditions of life are nearest the abysmal level of Asia or Africa; while in the British Isles it is the relatively non-industrialised Eire which has the lowest standard of living, generally speaking.

Not all industrial development is industrialisation. The difference is important because the industrial changes, which are undoubtedly taking place in many parts of Africa under various financial and technical aid schemes of the western powers, are, in fact, designed to strengthen the grip of imperialism and to step up the robbery and exploitation of the country receiving the "aid".

Throughout Africa western governments have been sinking millions of pounds to develop transport and communications. One has only to travel in Africa—or merely look at a map of the main railways—to realise how much effort is needed to provide Africa with adequate lines of communication and transport. If one takes West Africa as an example, it is clear that a crying need of this region is the development of rails and roadways which will connect these countries with one another (up to now, the main roads and railways have simply run from key centres of mineral production or market-assembly of cash crops down to the seaports, where foreign ships take these goods aboard for export to the west). A further need of these regions is the development of communications with their own hinterland, so as to help open up their own internal market, which the growth of their economy both demands and makes possible.

The independent states of West Africa are already discussing how to extend rail and road connections with one another, and, at the same time, are seeking to drive their communication lines deeper into their own interiors. Such steps are welcome and necessary. But parallel with such developments there are imperialist schemes to develop road and rail in Africa, not to assist Africa but, on the contrary, in order to facilitate the transport of wealth from Africa to the metropolitan centres of manufacture in Europe and the United States. Heavy western investments are being made, too, to increase the output of minerals in Africa. This also is not to "aid" Africa, but to rob her and aid the imperialists.

If the western powers have their way, the railways will continue to run straight from valuable ore-bearing mountains down to the seaports, so that millions of tons of rich minerals can be shipped away to the west—and the African landscape left flattened and derelict. This is happening, for example, with the rich iron ore in Liberia, in Mount Nimba, on the Guinea border. The Liberian-American-Swedish Minerals Company (L.A.M.C.O.) is investing £200 million to exploit this iron ore. To do this, they will build a 200-mile railway and harbour installations in order to carry the ore away. Similarly, a four-nation grouping of companies—Miferma (France, Britain, Italy and West Germany)—is constructing a 400-mile railway from Mauretania's rich, high-grade iron-ore deposits at Fort Gouraud down to the sea, at Port Etienne, where the harbour will be developed to take ships of up to 60,000 tons. To take this ore away, the eighteen-mile-long massif, rising to a height of 2,000 feet, is to be cut away. The manager of the mine has stated: "When we have finished, there will be no landscape." Precisely the same kind of thing is happening in Swaziland, where an agreement with Japan will lead to the building of a new railway to take away the iron ore.

Such developments bring no "aid" to Africa, nor will they assist her industrialisation. Real aid to Africa would consist in utilising this rich iron ore to establish iron and steel industries in Liberia, Guinea, Mauretania and Swaziland. But the big western firms extracting this mineral wealth have no interest in doing this. Their sole concern is how much profit can they make—and how quickly.

Some western economists call this robbery "aid" or "industrial development" or even "industrialisation". Scientifically speaking, however, *industrialisation means the construction of machines which can produce the means of production; that is to say, machines which can make machines and machine tools, so that a country can manufacture its own main requirements and not be dependent for them on some outside power. To produce its own machines, a country needs a modern engineering industry, and this, in its turn, requires its base in an iron and steel industry, electric power, and chemicals.* It is a striking commentary on the nature of the imperialist exploitation of Africa that after sixty years of western rule, the whole of Africa, apart from the white-dominated Union of South Africa, has no such industrial base.

But without industrialisation Africa cannot solve any of her problems. Industrialisation means farm machinery, electric power, fertilisers and insecticides which are necessary for modernising agriculture. Industrialisation means machines for light industry, thus making possible an increased output of consumer goods. Industrialisation means the creation of a skilled working class, an advance in education, technique and culture. Industrialisation leads to less heavy manual work and, by raising productivity, makes possible higher wages, better conditions and shorter hours. Industrialisation makes possible modern methods for building more schools and hospitals, and the rapid large-scale construction of housing. Industrialisation will expand the national income and the internal market, thus stimulating the all-round growth of the economy. Industrialisation will enable Africa to catch up the economically more advanced countries, to end her dependence on imperialism for machinery and spare parts, and to strengthen her national defences. Thus, in every way, industrialisation will improve the lives of the African people and help them to uphold their new-won national sovereignty.

No wonder the imperialists are opposed to the industrialisation of Africa.

At the time that British imperialism had to concede independence to Ghana that country had no national industries worth speaking of. She exported cocoa-beans, but imported cocoa products; exported timber but imported paper; exported palm-oil but imported soap; exported bauxite but imported aluminium ware. She even spent £5 million a year importing sacks into which to load her cocoa. Independent Ghana has begun to transform her economy, and to manufacture goods from her own raw materials. Ghana-produced tissue paper is, in fact, now being exported to other African countries, thus helping to disprove the argument that Ghana is not "suited" to manufacture but should limit herself to producing raw materials.

Sekou Toure stressed that in Guinea French imperialism had been concerned "to keep for itself the exclusive right in the sale of manufactured goods. Accordingly, it opposed all attempts at industrialisation." ("Towards Full Re-Africanisation": speech to the Congress of the Guinea Democratic Party, Conakry, 14 September 1959. *Presence Africaine*, pp. 43–4, Paris, 1959.)

This is the pattern throughout colonial and former colonial Africa. Even a country like Liberia, nominally independent for decades, suffers in the same way. It is said, for example, that when the Ducor Palace Hotel was constructed in Monrovia, every single item—apart from local stone—had to be imported, right down to the nails!

Many western economists have tried to advance "theories" to justify this warped international division of labour, in which Africa concentrates on the production of minerals and agricultural goods, selling them cheaply abroad and importing from the west manufactured goods and equipment at exorbitant prices.

Sometimes it is argued that Africa should first build up her infra-structure. At other times it is claimed that skilled workers and technicians must be trained first. Often the argument is simply reduced to the assertion that Africa will "always" be mainly a producer of agricultural items, or that she should rely on the extraction of her mineral wealth. It is even said that the existing iron-ore resources cannot provide the basis for an iron and steel industry because they are too far away from urban centres or from coal deposits.

So persistent are these attempts by the western powers to discourage industrialisation in Africa that one can scarcely pick up any official document in the west or read any article on Africa in the national press or economic journals without coming across some scornful reference to "prestige projects". African proposals to build a hydro-electric dam, or a new key factory, are often dismissed as "prestige building". But the luxury flats and hotels, the huge insurance offices and banks, owned by Europeans and still being constructed to serve European interests in many parts of Africa are ignored by these traducers of Africa's effort to reconstruct her economy.

But the west has not limited itself to pseudo-arguments. As long as it held direct sway over the territories of Africa it prevented every move towards industrialisation. This may seem a harsh judgment to some people, but facts are facts. A special United Nations Study on Economic Conditions in Non-Self Governing Territories (New York, 1958) has stated that the western met-ropolitan countries "provide only limited public financial assis-tance for the establishment and development of manufacturing industries in the territories under their administration". Figures available prove this claim up to the hilt. For example, out of the £148 million worth of funds provided under the United Kingdom Development and Welfare Act, between 1946 and 1956, less than ½ per cent was directly for industrial development. Similarly, the sums allocated under the first F.I.D.E.S. Plan for French overseas territories, for the period 1949–53, allowed less than ½ per cent for industrial development, while the estimates for the Belgian Congo's Ten Year Plan of 1949–59 did not even include industry as an item.

Clearly, this deliberate neglect of industry in Africa has not been purely a British policy; it has, we see, been pursued in

French and Belgian colonies, too, and it is followed at least as emphatically, if not more, by Spain and Portugal in "their" colonies. In other words, opposition to industrialisation is an essential element of colonialism, of the imperialist exploitation of Africa, and is a prime cause of the poverty and misery suffered by millions of Africans. Thus, the elimination of poverty and the creation of a truly national economy requires, as a first step, a drastic turn away from the imperialist policy of "no industrialisation".

The western powers still try to pursue this same policy of discouraging and delaying industrialisation in African territories even after they have won independence. Thus western "aid" schemes, and certainly the bulk of western investments, are directed towards the extractive industries, especially minerals. Western loans, not always forthcoming, not only carry heavy interest rates; more serious still, there is obviously a great reluctance on the part of western powers to make such loans available for real industrialisation. Loans to develop the infra-structure, mainly transport and communications, are made—for these make it easier for the imperialist monopolies to extract Africa's wealth. But loans to build an iron and steel base, or hydro-electric schemes—as the experience of Egypt and Ghana showed—are not so readily available. In fact, the World Bank Report for 1946–53 openly argues against loans for industrialisation, claiming that "Excessive emphasis on industry for industry's sake, above all, heavy industry, may leave an underdeveloped country with the symbol of development rather than the substance".

But heavy industry is not the "symbol" of development; it is its very "substance". Without heavy industry, Africa cannot really make fundamental economic and social progress. And that is precisely why the World Bank and other agencies dominated by imperialism discourage the industrialisation of Africa.

Precisely the same policy is pursued by the European Common Market powers towards the sixteen African Associated States, as has been noted above.

This explains the warnings given by President Nkrumah and other African leaders that the European Common Market is an instrument for maintaining Africa as a raw-materials appendage to the western powers and for preventing its industrialisation.

No one, least of all the leaders of the new African states, would pretend that the creation of a modern industrialised Africa will be an easy task. Technicians and skilled workers have to be trained, planning techniques developed, capital found and new enterprises constructed. And all this has to be done on the basis of a society in which there exist side by side remnants of primitive communal society, of early patriarchal slave society, of elementary feudalism and developing capitalism—and this entire complex dominated by a colonial economy which has restricted all normal growth and development.

Further, in planning for industrialisation the African states have to take care to allocate their present limited resources in a way which enables the maximum accumulation of capital for further all-round growth. They need to expand, diversify and modernise agriculture alongside industry. They need both heavy and light industry. They need to produce commodities on which at present they have to spend foreign exchange earnings. They need to plan for necessary wage increases while setting aside each year sufficient capital for investment and economic growth; and to allocate both for social services and for technical training. A headlong rush into industrialisation without considering all these other aspects of economic and social development would, of course, be reckless. Yet, without the clear goal of rapid industrialisation, much else would be without real purpose.

Appreciation of the key importance of industrialisation for the economic development of their countries is being shown by the African people and their organisations, as well as by the most advanced and most independent new states, such as Ghana, Guinea, Mali and the United Arab Republic. Thus Ghana is pressing ahead with its plans for the Volta Dam scheme, is planning to build 600 new factories, and is looking into the question of establishing an iron and steel base. The United Arab Republic, with Soviet assistance, is constructing the Aswan High Dam and other projects, and, again with Soviet help, is building Egypt's first cotton mill. Hitherto, all Egyptian cotton has had to be exported, mainly to the mills of western countries. Now Egypt will spin her own cotton. Her new mill is staffed by Egyptian engineers, technicians and skilled workers who have been specially trained in the U.S.S.R. Textile mills for Ghana, too, are one of the items listed in a Soviet-Ghana economic agreement. Similar industrial developments are planned for Mali and Guinea, and the Provisional Government for Algeria drew up plans for industrialisation even before Algeria gained its independence.

Most of the new African states have only been in existence a couple of years, some even less. One cannot therefore expect to see, as yet, any decisive change in the pattern of the economy in these countries. The change from an "underdeveloped" country to a developed one is a huge task. But the decisions of the All-African Peoples Conferences and of the gatherings of representatives of African states, as well as the plans of a number of individual African governments, show quite clearly that industrialisation is increasingly being seen as a main lever with which to overcome Africa's economic backwardness.

In this connection, there is special significance in the resolutions adopted by the Third All-African Peoples Conference which met at Cairo at the end of March 1961. Its resolution on democratic, economic and social development, which outlined a number of measures for overcoming the economic backwardness of Africa, emphasised the necessity for *the earliest possible creation of a heavy industry*.

Taking over Foreign-owned Enterprises

The building of a modern iron and steel base, electric power, engineering, chemical and fuel industries, will not be achieved overnight. Considerable resources need to be mobilised, capital accumulated and loans secured, and technicians and skilled workers trained. Important assets, such as minerals, communications, banking and insurance, which may still be in the hands of foreign monopolists, need, in one form or another, to be taken over by the independent African states themselves. This is a process which will help to strengthen the state sector of the economy and thus facilitate economic planning as well as defend national sovereignty.

Africa is already moving in this direction. Despite the wishes and activities of the western monopolies who would like to preserve the colonial character of Africa's economy, the laws of social development will undoubtedly determine Africa's march along the road to industrialisation and economic progress.

In Africa, where the economy is still so completely dominated by foreign monopolies, no real headway can be made without restricting and eventually uprooting foreign capital. As the new African states take over and start to put in hand measures to overcome their economic backwardness, they find that every important sector of their economy—minerals, agricultural products, trade, all forms of transport—railways, civil aviation, shipping—harbours and docks, banking and insurance, building and cement, electric power and processing factories—is dominated by, and sometimes completely in the hands of, big foreign companies.

This foreign possession of all the key points of the economy prevents the new states from planning their economic development, denies them the use of their natural resources to serve their own (and not overseas) interests and robs them of valuable capital which these resources can also earn in the form of exports. It is therefore understandable that increasingly voices are being raised in Africa demanding the nationalisation of foreign firms. This is shown, for example, in the resolutions of the Third All-African Peoples Conference which, amongst other things, call for "The nationalisation of the main plantations, banks, transport and insurance companies, industrial enterprises which belong to [foreign] organisations and imperialist agents."

The western powers always react most strongly against every threat to nationalise their properties, and they strive to tie the new African states to specific "no-nationalisation" pledges. At the same time, since a move against such companies is essential if complete independence is to be won, the newly established governments in Africa find it necessary to take certain measures in the direction of bringing the foreign concerns more closely under their control. Thus the Ghana Government took over the Cable and Wireless Company's interests on the expiry of the 1962 licence, took over the B.O.A.C. shares in the Ghana Airways, is buying out the Zim Navigation Company's shares in the Black Star Shipping Line, and has bought out five of the seven British-owned gold-mining companies in Ghana. In Nigeria airways and shipping have been nationalised, and there are demands for the taking over of cable and wireless[1] as well as of the major mining companies.

[1] The Nigerian Government is now taking steps to do this.

Similarly, in Guinea the government has been obliged, step by step, to bring the French and other foreign enterprises on its soil more under its control. In August 1960 a number of French banks in Guinea were compelled to cease operations. At the end of January 1961 two further French firms, the water supply company and the electricity company, were nationalised on the grounds that they had become "imperialist tools to undermine the Development Plan of the Guinean Republic". Diamond mining, too, was nationalised, and in August 1961 the French-owned Jules Burki Transport Company was nationalised. French insurance companies and a number of other firms have also been taken over.

Immediate nationalisation, whether with or without compensation, is not always the first step to be taken. Much depends on the sector of the economy in which the particular firm operates, on the size of the undertaking, its role in the total economy, the feeling and relations of forces within the country, including the attitude of the workers in the given enterprise, and also on the international situation. Measures being taken or advocated, short of direct take-over, are 51–49 ownership of shares and distribution of profits, a restriction on the export of profits, increased taxation of foreign firms, laws compelling a larger plough-back of profits into further capital developments, or wage laws compelling foreign firms to pay increased wages to their African employees. It was, incidentally, the refusal of the British gold-mining firms in Ghana to pay the new minimum wage which resulted in their being compulsorily bought out by the Ghana Government.

Whatever the specific step taken to curb the foreign monopolies, there is no slogan or procedure valid for every country and under all circumstances. The only valid standpoint is that the foreign economic strongholds must be attacked, weakened and eventually turned into national property. Failure to follow such a course can only menace the newly won national sovereignty and delay the country's development. But once the new African states embark on schemes of genuine economic development, steps against the foreign monopolies become inevitable; and even those governments in Africa which, at present, have no intention of moving against the foreign firms on their soil, will be compelled increasingly to do so by the logic of events.

The nationalisation of foreign firms also assists the development of a state sector of the economy, which is extremely important for African countries taking the path of independent development. In fact, in African countries where little industry exists, where the commanding heights of the economy are initially in the hands of foreign monopolies, and where, in the main, the African capitalist class is not rich enough or experienced enough (or even willing, its inclination being to seek wealth in the more familiar trading world rather than in tying up capital for longer-term interests), state initiative in developing the economy is essential. In such countries as Egypt, Ghana, Guinea or Nigeria, it is precisely the foreign undertakings which have been nationalised or bought out which create the basis for the state sector of the economy. But merely to take over the existing enterprises in an economy which has been deliberately held back and distorted by colonialism is insufficient; new enterprises, too, have to be built—iron and steel plants, electric power, oil refineries, engineering and cement factories and all the other components of modern industry.

State Sector and Economic Planning

The creation of these new enterprises, together with the further development of those taken over from the foreign monopolies, creates the necessity for economic planning by the state. Thus, a special feature of the new states in Africa is the initiation of economic plans. These plans are mainly plans for public capital expenditure, and contain little beyond hopes as far as the private sector (whether foreign or indigenous) is concerned. This, of course, is inevitable until all the main means of production become public property. Often the plans of the new states are extremely limited in conception and in no sense directed towards overcoming colonialism. For instance, in Togo, the Ivory Coast and the Malagasy Republic the main emphasis in the economic plans is on agriculture, and furthermore overwhelmingly directed towards export crops. Even the sums devoted to industry are related often to transport or mining—in both cases frequently serving to intensify the export of the natural resources in the interests of overseas firms. In the Republic of Sudan, plans for

1959–61 show two-fifths of government expenditure being devoted to agriculture and nearly two-fifths to transport.

A number of African states, however, are initiating more ambitious plans which will help to transform the character of their economies. In Ghana a key project is the Volta River scheme. As originally conceived, this is to be a comprehensive scheme, providing cheap and abundant electric power for a wide variety of industries, establishing local aluminium production, creating new urban areas, irrigating large areas of land and so making possible an expansion of agricultural production and a diversification of crops, including foodstuffs and additional industrial crops and the foundation of a cattle industry, and lastly the creation of a large artificial lake in which fish could be produced for local consumption, and on which lake transport could be developed. Decisive headway with this scheme is scheduled to take place under the new Seven-Year Plan.

For several years the Ghana Government strove to raise funds in the west for the Volta scheme, only to find similar delays and obstacles as those met with by the United Arab Republic over the Aswan Dam. It is not without significance that the first major offer from the west, namely a £30 million loan towards the building of the Akosombo Dam and power plant, was only made after the Ghana parliamentary delegation visited the Soviet Union; and the later American offer of funds, in 1961, to help build the smelter followed the decision of the Soviet Government to help construct the Bui Dam, on the Black Volta, and was made concurrently with President Nkrumah's visit to the Soviet Union and other socialist countries. In fact, the *Guardian* (12 August 1961) said that United States backing was only forthcoming because the U.S. State Administration "feared that Ghana would fall straight into the Communist camp if it failed to secure Western finance for the project". This is an illustration of what Mr. Khrushchov has termed "indirect Soviet aid"—that is, the compulsion of the western powers to give loans for projects on which they are not too keen, simply out of fear that the country concerned might otherwise seek such aid from the socialist countries.

In Ghana, in addition to the Volta scheme, the 1959–64 Plan (now to be replaced by a new Seven-Year Plan) allows for the establishment of 600 new factories, producing a range of 100 products. These factories were to have been built largely by private enterprise, both foreign and Ghanaian, and steps have been taken to encourage such development. In practice, however, the government's Industrial Development Corporation (I.D.C.) has found it necessary to initiate much of the factory development itself. Its report for 1960 gave a total of 54 industrial plants operating in 42 different industries, with a further 22 under construction or already approved and a further 31 awaiting examination or approval. A number of these new factories are owned 100 per cent by the I.D.C. and in many others the I.D.C. has shares. The factories cover the production of nails, furniture and timber products, matches, boats, bricks, soap, cigars, biscuits and other light industries.

In 1962 Ghana made further important progress with its industrial programme. Of significance are the establishment of factories for secondary processing which will enable Ghana to cut down on her imports of certain goods which she can now produce herself. These include plants for aluminium sheets and utensils, for paints and insecticides, and a factory producing jute bags at Kumasi, right in the heart of the cocoa-producing area. Further plans include a £1,700,000 steel plant, a cocoa-processing factory, a tobacco-drying plant, a cannery for processing tuna fish, a £1,600,000 factory for bleaching, dyeing and printing grey baft, two shoe factories and four fruit and vegetable canneries.

Some of the new plants are foreign owned, such as the United Africa Company truck assembly plant at Tema; others will be joint ventures, with the Ghana Government and foreign companies acting as partners (for example, the Government-Philips radio assembly firm of Nassar Ltd. near Accra, and the Ghana-Japanese project to establish a vehicle assembly plant); and finally, the Ghana Government itself is establishing a number of its own state enterprises. Ghanaian private capital is expected to play a less important role, mainly concentrating on small enterprises.

Ghana is clearly passing beyond what has been termed the "beer, boots and bricks" stage, but experience already shows that Ghanaian private capital is incapable of industrialising the country. State initiative, state planning and the building of a state sector are becoming the essential core of all the republic's industrial plans. This, together with the widespread development of agricultural co-operatives and the establishment of state farms, alongside economic co-operation with socialist countries, will assist Ghana to avoid the normal capitalist path of development.

Is Western Capital Essential?

One of the arguments spread in the west, and accepted in some government circles in the new African states, is that the economy of African states cannot be developed without western capital and western advice. In some ways this conception is the main ideological weapon of the imperialist powers, a means by which their neo-colonialist tactic can be pursued and the African states and peoples still robbed of their full emancipation. Acting in accordance with this belief in the indispensability of western "aid", some African states make concessions and offer special inducements in order to attract western investments. In fact, the idea of investments from the west is often given priority over loans.

Of course, it is not suggested that African states should sever all their economic relations with the west. Such a course would be both absurd and impractical. But Africa's economic relations with the imperialist powers can only be of real and lasting benefit to Africa if the old pattern of relations is changed and Africa's economic dependence on the west ended. Heavy dependence on western investments can be a real danger to Africa. As President Nkrumah has rightly warned:

"Private foreign investment from abroad is . . . open to a number of objections. First, the private investor naturally wishes to make as large a profit as possible and the types of industry and trade in which the largest profits can be made are not necessarily the ones which would serve the interests of Ghana. . . . Secondly, the foreign investor naturally wishes to export as much of his profit as possible to his own home country. Our interest is that profit from industry should be ploughed back into Ghana so as to develop further industry.

Finally, if we rely exclusively or even largely upon private foreign investment for our industrialisation, we would in fact become politically and economically dependent upon expatriate interests. Indeed, all we should be doing would be to reintroduce colonialism in another guise."

(Broadcast to the nation, 22 December 1961.)

This danger is underlined by Nigeria's Six-Year Plan, 1962 to 1968. This is a most ambitious plan, and will, if achieved, make a considerable contribution to Nigeria's economic progress. It envisages the spending of no less than £1,200 million over the six years, and includes the important Niger Dam scheme (£68 million) which will assist agriculture, fishing and navigation as well as providing electric power; an iron and steel complex for which £30 million is allocated; a big expansion of transport and of agriculture, including the increased production of food crops; a state development bank and insurance company; an oil refinery; and the large-scale training of skilled personnel, for which £70 million will be provided, compared with under £19 million in the previous five-year plan drawn up by the colonial authorities. All these projects are commendable. The problems arise, however, when one considers the financing of this plan. In the first place, out of the £1,200 million total, nearly half, £535 million, is expected from private funds, most of it foreign. Over the next two years alone it is estimated that no less than £176 million foreign investments will pour into Nigeria. Much of this will be in oil (the refinery, in fact, will be mainly a Shell project); and a number of foreign firms are concerned with the iron and steel project. Thus new major giants of Nigerian industry will be largely in foreign hands.

Furthermore, of the £675 million which the Nigerian Government expects to obtain from public funds, about half—£339 million—is anticipated in the form of grants and loans from abroad. Whether Nigeria will obtain loans and grants of such dimensions is itself very doubtful. But the combination of heavy dependence on foreign investments and reliance on western loans could be a real danger. Even *The Economist* (7 July 1962) remarks that "this dependence on foreign aid . . . is a reminder of how much the country depends upon decisions taken elsewhere". And such decisions, of course, could lead to complete neo-colonialist control of Nigeria and the virtual loss of her national independence.

Commenting on the high level of anticipated foreign investment in Nigeria in the next two years, *The Economist* (7 July 1962) asks: "Can any African government, in the turbulent and uncertain state of African politics today, comfortably look forward to a time when the bulk of its industry will be in foreign hands?" And it warns that there is a risk of "violent political reaction" if the funds, and hence the control of these new projects, are not in Nigerian hands. On the other hand, if the Nigerian Government suggests public participation in these new enterprises, and even, as in the case of the oil refinery, a majority holding, then, says *The Economist*, "foreign companies draw back and look over their shoulders for the expropriators' axe". This dilemma underlines the dangers of excessive dependence on western investments.

No continent or country believes in complete autarchy, in the conception of a territory being so completely economically self-sufficient that it has no economic relations with anyone else. Africa needs economic relations with other regions and with other countries. The only question is: On what basis should Africa have such relations? If Africa is to win its economic independence then relations with the west cannot be on the basis of an industrialised metropolis exploiting Africa's raw materials and dominating its market; not on the basis of African resources and trade being in the hands of American and Western European monopolies; nor on the basis of the European Common Market, with Africa a hewer of wood and a drawer of water for European industry. Africa, to win its economic independence, will expect and will demand economic relations on the basis of African ownership of Africa's resources, on the basis of equality and mutual benefit, on the basis of fair prices and normal trading relations. But to achieve this, Africa must become a modern, industrialised region—and this, at least in the initial stages, requires more than the domestic effort of the new African states, even more than the combined domestic effort of the whole African continent. It requires machines and trained technicians and to obtain these Africa has the great advantage of being able to establish closer economic relations with the socialist world.

Socialist Aid

Many African countries, including Ghana, Guinea, Mali, Egypt, Tunisia, Morocco, Somalia, Libya and Ethiopa, already have economic agreements with the Soviet Union and other socialist countries. More recently, Senegal, Cameroun and Dahomey have signed agreements with a number of socialist countries. The socialist world is a growing factor in Africa's progressive development. Already the socialist sector leads the world in many fields of science and technology. By 1970 it will account for considerably more than half of the world's total production. The emergence of the socialist camp has meant the ending of the monopoly which the western powers previously enjoyed in the export of machinery and in the training of technicians.

Socialist economic agreements are based on complete equality between the two parties. There are no strings attached to such agreements, as has been stressed by Nasser, Sekou Toure and Nkrumah. Socialist credits are provided at $2\frac{1}{2}$ per cent interest, in place of the 6 or 7 per cent usually asked for by the west. The credits are provided direct to governments, and not to private industry; and the consequence is that the state sector of the economy of the recipient country is strengthened, planning is made more easy, and resources can be directed where they are most needed. In addition, socialist credits or loans are repayable over a long term, either in the currency of the recipient country or in its traditional exports; in no case does a socialist country demand repayment in dollars or other western currencies. All blueprints and patents are provided free. Technicians for new enterprises are usually trained in the course of construction so that by the time the new factory starts operations new technicians in the country concerned can take over control. Socialist loans go, in particular, to help industrial development. The Soviet Union alone is building some 480 major projects in underdeveloped countries, including hydro-electric dams and iron and steel plants. Whole plants are exported to Africa by the Soviet Union, Poland, Czechoslovakia, the German Democratic Republic and other socialist countries—but when the machinery is installed and operations begin, not one penny profit is taken out because not a single penny of socialist money is invested; the whole factory belongs to the recipient African country itself. Such economic relations, in contrast to those which the western powers try to foist on Africa, are of direct assistance to Africa's economic growth and independence.

Even discounting for the moment the character of the aid made available by the socialist countries as contrasted to the use to which western funds and investments are put, it is instructive to look at the quantity of aid now coming from the socialist countries. Even the account submitted to the United States Congress on 29 August 1962, on economic grants and loans extended to the underdeveloped countries between mid-1955 and the end of 1961, shows that the United States provided $502 million to Africa, while what it terms the "Sino-Soviet bloc" provided $601 million. It is well known that American calculations of "aid" to underdeveloped countries usually lump together military aid, economic assistance for "defence support", tied loans for the purposes of purchasing surplus U.S. goods and services, and other items which make no contribution towards the economic development of the emergent nations. U.S. overseas investments, too, are often included in "aid" totals. But even apart from this, the United States can no longer argue that socialist aid is "negligible" and makes no serious impact on the economic growth of the underdeveloped countries. On the contrary, socialist aid, both in character and in scale, is becoming a significant feature of our present epoch.

The experience of all the countries in the socialist camp, and now of Cuba, too, shows that far from dependence on western capital being necessary for economic progress, reliance on internal resources together with economic co-operation with socialist countries is the main basis on which economic growth can be stimulated.

But economics is not simply a question of planning and utilising inanimate resources, a matter of funds, raw materials, machines and statistics. All progress depends on people, and economic progress in an economically backward region like Africa requires an exceptional effort by the people. Thus economic expansion requires democratic expansion. The immense economic tasks facing Africa demand the utmost mobilisation of the people, of their labour, their talents, their skill, their enthusiasm —and this is only possible if there is the fullest democracy, with complete trade union and political rights for workers, including the right to strike, trade union independence from government or party control, and the right for the working class to form its own independent political party.

In addition to democratic liberties the workers and peasants will expect to receive increased benefits from the economy which they are helping to expand. Sacrifices in the national interest they are prepared to make, but they cannot be expected to make all the sacrifices while they see a new ruling class grabbing for itself all the privileges and pickings made possible by the labour of the masses. Those who think in terms of large cars, £100,000 mansions and "golden beds" should remember the lesson of Ghana; the awakened people of Africa will not lightly exchange their old rulers for new ones. They have struggled, fought and died for a new Africa, for an Africa free and independent, for an Africa of prosperity and progress. For such an Africa the people will work with a new will and spirit; for such an Africa the people will accept temporary hardships and shortcomings. But those who try to sit on top of the masses, who try to keep the workers and peasants "in their proper place", and endeavour to abrogate to themselves all the power and privileges of the new state, will have a short political life; for the people of Africa are resolved that economic independence and economic advance is not to be for the purpose of building Africa in the image of the western world, a world of rich and poor, of economic and political power in the hands of an upper crust, but an Africa in which the economic resources will at last be returned to the African people and utilised in their interests.

CHAPTER FOUR

DEMOCRACY AND THE ONE-PARTY SYSTEM

Although the various sessions of the All-African Peoples Conference have adopted no special resolutions on the question of democracy, the very aims of the national independence movements embrace the whole concept of the political rights and power of the African people as against the former colonial power. Moreover, the struggles against colonial rule have only been possible because the leaders of the national organisations have mobilised the people, built political parties and trade unions and other democratic organisations and, in a most profound fashion, awakened millions of formerly dormant people to political discussion and activity. Thus, in its very essence, the national liberation movement is a democratic movement.

Those African states which have won political independence are now considering what further steps should be taken to strengthen their national sovereignty, reconstruct their economies and reorganise their social life. This can only be done with the help of the people; and to ensure that the people are drawn into this effort and that de-colonisation is completed, the utmost development of democracy is required.

In a speech in January 1962 Sekou Toure stressed that the enormous tasks facing Africa required "the complete mobilisation of all the intellectual and physical, moral and material forces of the people", and that therefore the Democratic Party of Guinea was introducing "the widest and most profound democratic methods as the main condition".

Under colonial rule democracy was denied to the African people—and in many territories still under European domination, such as Angola, Mozambique and smaller Portuguese enclaves and islands, in the Republic of South Africa, in the Rhodesias—little is allowed, if anything, in the way of democratic rights. For these territories the first phase of struggle, to end foreign rule, has still to be carried through; and in the course of such a struggle, as the people become more united and the forces of those engaged in battle increase, so will the possibility arise of certain democratic rights, certain concessions being gained even before the winning of independence. Under certain conditions the securing of such vantage points can be of great help to the movement, widening the arena of struggle, allowing the use of various legal forms of action, and opening the way to still more significant advances.

In many of these territories the slogan is "one man, one vote". In the context of Africa, this just demand has a two-fold significance. The slogan has arisen, especially in territories where there has been considerable white settlement, to meet two injustices. It has been the practice of colonialism, especially British colonialism, when forced in recent years to retreat and allow some voting rights to Africans, to restrict the power of African votes in two ways. In the first place, there is the system of separate voting rolls, under which the European settlers are able to vote for their own European candidates, even where the settlers are an absolute minority of the population; and a separate lower roll exists for Africans. Of course, it is not put as crudely as this. The division as between European and African rolls is covered up by various educational and property qualifications which the colonial authorities have couched in such a form that they are bound to ensure an absolute minimum of Africans on the upper roll. Thus the first swindle in colonial-run elections in Africa is one of *race* discrimination, of the African majority being compelled to allow the election by the white minority of a number of European members of assemblies, quite out of proportion to their numbers in the country. Accompanying this race discrimination is *class* discrimination, which is even carried over, for a time, in the newly independent states after the national discrimination has been lessened, or abolished. This class discrimination is exercised by the education and property income qualifications which usually exclude the overwhelming majority of workers and peasants from the franchise, and thus make possible the domination of the new legislative assemblies and parliaments by representatives of the African bourgeoisie and petty bourgeoisie.

The demand for one man, one vote, therefore, is a demand to end both racial and class discrimination in the franchise.

One need only to look at the figures for registration as well as actual voting to see how many African people are still excluded from voting in a number of African territories. In the Portuguese territories in Africa the ban on African voting rights is almost complete; in any case, the Salazar fascist system makes any voting here a mockery. In the Republic of South Africa Africans have no right to vote, neither for African candidates (who are not allowed to stand, in any case) nor for Europeans. In Southern and Northern Rhodesia the present sharp phase of conflict is very closely connected with the battle by the African people to win full voting rights. In the November 1958 Federal elections, for example, the actual registration of Africans for the vote was 642 in Southern Rhodesia, 89 in Northern Rhodesia and 16 in Nyasaland—a total of 747 out of an African population of some 7 million. In Kenya, too, the franchise is limited by education and property; in the last general elections there were only some 800,000 votes in a country of nearly 9 million population.

Of course voting rights are only one aspect of the struggle of the African people for democracy, but, understandably in those territories which do not yet enjoy political independence, the right to vote, the right to universal manhood suffrage, is a key demand. At the same time a struggle is being waged for freedom of meeting, of press, and of association in both the political and trade union fields. Even in those colonial territories in Africa where some of these rights may already exist in a formal sense, in practice they are constantly interfered with, parties are suppressed, national leaders arrested, strikes outlawed and a variety of forms of police supervision and intimidation introduced so as to hamper the people's efforts to secure justice. Amongst examples in recent years one can mention the outlawing of the National Democratic Party in Southern Rhodesia;[1] the arrests at the end of 1961 of nearly 3,000 people in Northern Rhodesia including more than 2,000 members of the United National Independence

[1] And, more recently, of the Zimbabwe African People's Union.

Party whose activities have been severely restricted by the authorities; and the arrest of Nelson Mandela and other African leaders in South Africa.

Democracy and the New African States

In the independent African states, however, the battle for democracy has reached a new stage and poses a whole series of new problems. In the first case, the winning of political independence, although it represents an important advance and provides a jumping-off ground for further progress, does not automatically abolish all the relics of colonialism. All the anti-democratic laws remain for a time on the statute books, and some of the anti-democratic practices built into the former imperialist state machine continue, especially as European cadres of this state apparatus are often retained for a considerable period after the winning of independence. Thus, it was only in January 1962 that the Ghana Government formally removed the ban on the import of a number of progressive publications, although it is only fair to state that, in practice, the Ghana Government for some considerable time turned a blind eye to this decree.

In addition to specific anti-democratic laws and practices, and the retention, for a time, of officials of the former regime, the actual constitutions which the newly independent states inherit have been drawn up in agreement with the former colonial power and naturally, therefore, bear the imprint of colonialism to a considerable extent. State structure, parliamentary procedure, legal system, powers of police—all, in process of time, will be found to be inadequate for the aims of the new states, for eliminating colonialism and building up flourishing economies. That is why the Africanisation of the state apparatus becomes a major demand in all new African states, and why these states increasingly find it necessary to change the constitution imposed upon them.

In the field of local government, too, fundamental changes are needed. The colonial system, twisting traditional African authorities to its own purpose, established forms of indirect rule and of "Native Administration" which utilised feudal chieftains, converted chiefs, or appointed new ones, to act as paid civil servants of colonialism, and even set up systems of local rule through chiefs where none had previously existed.

Such institutions have been found by the new African states to be a barrier to further progress, and an obstacle to the democratic activity of the people. This has been especially the case with the feudal rulers of Northern Nigeria, with the chiefs of Ashanti in Ghana, and with the system of chiefs in Guinea. In the latter case the progressive forces represented in the Democratic Party of Guinea found it necessary at a very early stage— even before independence was won—to take decisive steps to destroy the former power of the chiefs and to introduce instead a widespread system of village democracy. This action, taken during the period of the operation of the French *Loi Cadre* (outline law), undoubtedly was a key factor in securing Guinea's overwhelming "No" vote to De Gaulle in 1958.

In contrast to Guinea was the outcome of the referendum in Niger. Here, too, the government under the progressive leadership of the Sawaba Party, led by Prime Minister Djibo Bakary, campaigned for a "No" vote. Unfortunately, nothing had been done in Niger to break the power of the chiefs, who, in consequence, were able to influence the peasants to vote "Yes". In addition, since the chiefs controlled the countryside, they also controlled the voting and vote-counting machine and were thus able to turn even "No" votes into "Yes". Thus Niger did not opt for independence in 1958, the progressive government fell, and Djibo Bakary and other Sawaba Party leaders had to go into exile.

In Mali, too, the power of the chiefs has been clipped. "We have given the villages an elected council," explains Madeira Keita, Mali Minister of the Interior. "Naturally we have specified the functions of the chief, whom the government retains the right to nominate on the advice of the elected council, so that the chief can do nothing without consulting it." (*The Voice of Africa:* October 1961.)

In Ghana, also, the government and the Convention People's Party were compelled, in defence of their newly won independence, to take strong action against the chiefs in Ashanti and, in Ghana as a whole, restrict power chiefly through the establishment of new machinery of local government and through setting up new institutions which, while allowing the chiefs certain rights, brought them effectively under the government. But the chiefs of Ghana are still there, and some impression of their still existing influence, wealth and power could be gained from their extravagant display at the time of the visit of the Queen at the end of 1961. In Nigeria, too, it is clear that the power of the feudal rulers in the north will have to be decisively broken before a fundamental advance can be made by Nigeria's 40 million people.

Pre-Colonial Traditions

While taking steps to weaken the powers of this former ruling caste, the African people are not unmindful of the fact that traditionally their tribal life included many important democratic practices which not even colonial rule has been able entirely to destroy. In the pre-colonial era, for example, there were parts of Africa in which the development of a state apparatus, of weapons of coercion and a professional army, had not taken place. Even where the state had developed, the apparatus of coercion was relatively small; the functions of the state, for managing the collective interests, for defence against external enemies, for the organisation of public works and collective labour, the control and distribution of food reserves in case of need, were mainly carried out through moral pressure, custom and a recognition of common interests.

"In many African societies", says Jean Suret-Canale, "there were no chiefs with permanent powers over the members of the community." The land chief had the function of allocating the commonly owned land to the members of the community, and of carrying out various religious or magic rites to ensure a successful harvest; and the war chiefs had rights in his special sphere, but even these were limited in their character and in duration. Outside of these functions the chief was an individual like everyone else, with few privileges and no rights over other members of the community. In fact, the responsibilities of his position often put the chief at a disadvantage compared with the rest of his people. In times of catastrophe, such as floods or drought, the chief who was responsible for ensuring good harvests could be stripped of his position, or even killed. Among some peoples, such as the Yorubas, kingship was restricted to a certain period of time which was usually terminated by the killing of the king—a practice, incidentally, which was followed in other societies outside Africa.

No one would pretend that pre-colonial Africa presented an idyllic picture, yet there were already in existence certain democratic forms of government which even colonial rule has not completely buried. Lord Hailey has stressed that "It is rare to find in British Colonial Africa any instance in which the indigenous form of rule previously in force could be described as autocratic." (*Native Administration in the British African Territories:* Part IV, H.M.S.O. 1951, p. 2.) The individual chiefs, he points out, had no machinery of force to secure obedience to their orders; their ultimate sanction lay in securing the agreement of the traditional advisers "and ultimately of the community itself". Moreover, the powers of the community were not limited to ones of passive acceptance or refusal of instructions; they had the right, as a community, to unseat or "de-stool" the chiefs.

The same point has been admitted by Kenneth Bradley, who, writing in an official government publication, *Britain's Purpose in Africa*, has pointed out that the chief could seldom decide anything "except on the advice of his council, which was itself closely bound by the will of the common people as expressed at village meetings".

But there was another aspect of tribal democracy, one which had significance for present-day Africa, and that is the method by which the community discussed its problems and arrived at a solution to them. The whole purpose of the discussions was not to secure a victory for "one side" over "the other" but to consider every aspect of the problem, to let every viewpoint be heard and be taken into account so as to reach a decision which was acceptable to all and which could be put into effect with the full backing of the people. In other words, tribal democracy involved a search for unanimity, for the highest common factor of agreement, and not a clash of two conflicting views or "two parties".

There was, of course, essentially nothing different between these democratic practices of African tribal society—popular control of the chief and democratic discussion to reach unanimity—and those followed by tribal societies in other regions of the world. Thus, in describing Lewis H. Morgan's findings on the Iroquois gens, Engels writes: "The gens has a council, the democratic assembly of all adult male and female members of the gens, all with equal voice. This council elected and deposed the sachems [headmen in times of peace] and war chiefs and, likewise, the remaining 'Keepers of the Faith'. . . . In short, it was the sovereign power in the gens."

Morgan himself said: "All the members of an Iroquois gens were personally free, and they were bound to defend each other's freedom; they were equal in privileges and in personal rights, the sachem and the chiefs claiming no superiority. . . . Liberty, equality and fraternity, though never formulated, were cardinal principles of the gens." (*Origin of the Family, Private Property and the State.*)

In other words, the practice of African tribes of leaving ultimate powers in the hands of the community is not a specific *African* feature, as some western commentators tend to imply, but a common feature of tribal forms of society everywhere.

The same applies to the method of discussion common in pre-colonial Africa. Engels explains that among the Iroquois gens the tribal council sat in public, surrounded by other members of the tribe, who had the right to join in the discussion and have their opinions heard. It was open to everyone present to address the council, though women could only do so through a spokesman of their choice. The final decisions were made by the council, but, stresses Engels, among the Iroquois "the final decision had to be adopted unanimously"; and he adds the point that this principle was also widespread among the German mark communities. Even when tribal councils joined into a federal council the principle that decisions had to be unanimous was still retained.

The same principles were observed by early Greek tribes. Engels points out that at the time of Homer the popular assembly (*agora*) was convened to decide all important matters. At the assembly every man had the right to speak, and the decision was made by show of hands or by acclamation. The assembly's decisions, said Engels, were "sovereign and final". G. F. Scho-mann, in his *Antiquities of Greece*, wrote: "Whenever a matter is discussed that requires the co-operation of the people for its execution, Homer gives us no indication of any means by which the people could be forced to it against their will." It was only later, with the development of slavery and the creation of a class society, that the institutions of force, of a state, arose, and that the sovereign power of the people was swept away.

More recently President Sukarno has emphasised that in ancient Indonesia, too, there was no practice and no tradition of a majority and an opposition. "Our nation," he said, "in its lower levels and echelons, in the villages and communities evolved, centuries ago, its own democratic methods. Rather than the idea of democratic majority and opposition, our society has evolved for itself the ideas of democratic consultation and unanimity. . . ."

Although, as the years passed, the forms in which these early expressions of democracy were practised may have acquired certain specific African features, basically such democratic procedures were not something peculiar to Africa but a certain stage of development through which all peoples have passed.

In Africa imperialist rule shattered the traditional forms of economy and introduced the system of twentieth-century colonialism. As part of this process, it transformed the previous forms of tribal democracy, robbing them of their democratic content though still making use of their outward forms. This was the essence of the system of indirect rule. Where elementary feudalism was more advanced, and the chiefs had already assumed certain autocratic powers, as, for example, in Northern Nigeria or Uganda, it was easier to ensure that the democratic rights and activity of the people were limited. But nowhere did the people lightly accept the imperialist-imposed forms of local rule or "Native Administration", and it is significant that in those independent African states which are most advanced serious steps have been taken to cut back the arbitrary powers which chiefs had generally obtained under colonial rule, and to establish democratic forms and procedures inspired by the same human hopes that gave rise to traditional concepts of democracy. It is not without interest that Engels, in giving his positive appraisal of the democratic content of early tribal society, closes his book with this quotation from Lewis H. Morgan's *Ancient Society*:

"Democracy in government, brotherhood in society, equality in rights and privileges, and universal education, foreshadow the next higher plane of society to which experience, intelligence and knowledge are steadily tending. *It will be a revival, in a higher form, of the liberty, equality and fraternity of the ancient gentes.*"

One- or Two-Party System?

What forms of democratic government are emerging in the new Africa? And how will they evolve further in the coming period? Many commentators in the western world—and this unfortunately goes even for some well-intentioned people—look at African political structures through western eyes. This is especially so in Britain where "the Westminster model", the two-party system, and the principle of the official Opposition are propounded as if they were synonymous with the very term "democracy". But the people of Africa are not firmly wedded to this idea. While amongst sections of the rising African capitalist class and petty bourgeoisie there is a certain tendency to copy some of the worst features of western forms of democracy and government, especially in the realms of parliamentary procedure, the experience of trying to make use of political independence to solve the serious economic and social problems which have been left as the grim heritage of the colonial system is convincing the African people, their organisations and their most outstanding leaders, that western forms of democracy do not necessarily have much relevance in Africa's present circumstances. This was clearly brought out in the discussions in March 1959 at a seminar held at Ibadan, Nigeria, on "Representative Government and National Progress", in which delegates from a number of different African territories took part.

Although this was a discussion conference and no binding conclusions were reached or decisions taken, the deliberations clearly showed that "nobody wanted merely to take over institutions inherited from the colonising powers; everybody considered that there must be changes and adaptations and that newly independent countries must not be expected to govern themselves in the images of the European powers". (*West Africa*, 11 April 1959.)

The inadequacy of the institutions of European capitalism for newly independent states has been sharply emphasised by President Sukarno of Indonesia in terms which have considerable relevance to the situation in Africa. Speaking at the University of Istanbul in April 1959 he said:

"We imitated the practice of Western countries in establishing a pattern of parliamentary liberal democracy which came straight from the text-books of Western Europe and America. . . . We swallowed it and got violent indigestion. . . . The sickness grew worse, not better, and eventually it began to menace not only the health, but even the very life of the nation. . . . Something had to be done. We had to apply our own system of democracy, which is in harmony with the character of our nation. . . . We had to make it possible for all sections of our society to participate in the function of government."

The essence of many of the discussions now taking place in Africa and the west regarding democracy in Africa tends to centre around the question of the two-party system and the official Opposition. Many western commentators, in recent times, have spoken in critical terms of the trend in the new African states towards one-party systems, and in doing so have often placed indiscriminately in one basket states where wide-spread democratic discussion and activity take place, and those where extreme arbitrariness and repression reign. The government of Ghana, in particular, has come in for much criticism from such quarters, and totally misleading slogans such as "Black dictatorship" have been freely used in the British press to describe the situation in that country.

It can be argued that the one-party system is to an extent a return to or a continuation of traditional forms of African democracy in that it excludes the conception of an official opposition, of a majority and a minority. But it is not simply that. In many parts of Africa there have sprung up national parties which are the voice of the whole people and have expressed their national demands and aspirations during the struggle for political independence. Such parties embrace workers and peasants, intellectuals and petty bourgeois sections, national capitalists and even sometimes chiefs; and within the ranks of such parties all patriotic and anti-colonial classes are united around the common aim of overthrowing the rule of the colonial power.

Experience has taught the people that the utmost unity of their forces is essential for this task; and thus have arisen such mass parties as the Sudanese Union of Mali, the Democratic Party of Guinea, the Convention People's Party of Ghana, the United National Independence Party of Northern Rhodesia, the Zimbabwe African People's Union of Southern Rhodesia, the Malawi Congress of Nyasaland, the Tanganyika African National Union—all of them mass parties, uniting the overwhelming majority of the people for anti-imperialist and independent aims.

In a sense these mass parties are more than political parties in the normal meaning of the term; they are the national united fronts of their respective countries. In the conditions of Africa, however, where class forces are still in a process of formation, where the mobility between classes is considerable, where many workers are migrants or conscripted peasants and where many peasants are casual workers, where peasants become small traders and their sons become intellectuals, where a new bourgeoisie is even now arising from the ranks of the bigger traders and richer farmers and even from amongst those petty bourgeois forces which utilise their political positions to acquire new economic strength—under such conditions it is, perhaps, natural that mass national organisations should arise at this stage rather than specific, clearly defined class parties.

What has provoked the discussion, however, is not simply that all the healthy forces of the nation have combined in order to win independence, but that *after* independence has been won and new African governments have been formed and states established, the overwhelming dominance of one party remains. Thus in independent Guinea, Mali, Ghana and Tanganyika, for example, there is a one-party system. How do African leaders look at this problem? What is their view? And is it possible to equate such systems with democracy? In reply to this latter question, many western commentators would assert "No!" But African political leaders and thinkers claim that their one-party systems are in no sense a denial of democracy.

Julius Nyerere, for example, leader of the Tanganyika African National Union, states:

"We have a one-party government, to all intents and purposes a one-party state. Although our National Assembly is the same shape as the House of Commons, T.A.N.U. members sit facing as well as behind the Government benches. We make no provision for payment to the 'Leader of the Opposition' and we use Government machinery to explain the purposes of the T.A.N.U. Government to the people, and the T.A.N.U. machinery to explain Government policy. . . . Yet I believe that Tanganyika is a thoroughly democratic country."
(*East Africa and Rhodesia:* 7 December 1961.)

In an interview (published in *National Guardian,* 18 September 1961) Nyerere explained that to him democracy in a poverty-stricken and recently colonial country means a united, single-minded effort for the rapid economic, social and cultural betterment of all its people. Thus presumably anything which disturbs this united effort and hampers or delays the betterment of the people cannot be regarded as working for democracy.

The same points have been stressed by Madeira Keita, Mali's Minister of the Interior.

"For us the essential thing is to mobilise all the forces of the country to move forward. . . . Does democracy necessarily imply more than one party? We say no. . . . At the present moment in African history there is no need to multiply parties, there is no need to give oneself the luxury of sterile and fratricidal opposition, there is no need to give ourselves a ministerial crisis every three months if we have decided to go for independence, to consolidate the independence of the African states and if we want to achieve unity and speedily raise Africa from the economic and cultural point of view to the level of other countries and other peoples."
(*The Voice of Africa:* October 1961.)

The point has been put even more sharply by Ndabaningi Sithole who has underlined very emphatically the dangers for the new African states of an Opposition which can in reality be the pawn of imperialism and a weapon to disrupt the people's efforts to overcome the remnants of colonialism.

"The recently emancipated African countries do not place great importance on the two-party system, partly because it does not in itself guarantee democratic processes and partly because, at this particular stage of their development, and when it is realised that the former *master* countries are only too eager to return by hook or by crook, the Opposition may only be African in appearance but European in fact. The Opposition may have its remote controls in London, Washington, D.C., or in Paris."
(*The Voice of Africa:* September 1961.)

Thus the main consideration in the minds of African national leaders is the *preservation of national unity* to prevent the return of colonialism, to scotch the neo-colonialist endeavours and practices of the imperialist powers, and to build up the nation; and the *form* which experience has tended to show to be the most suitable for these tasks, in certain African territories, is that of the single mass party.

Sithole rightly warns, however, that the new African states cannot ensure democracy solely by following a one-party system. "Neither it nor the two-party system can guarantee democracy to the peoples of Africa and to the peoples of the world. The two-party system may be European imperialism's gateway to African countries, and, equally so, the one-party system may be dictatorship's first eggs in Africa." There is no special virtue, in principle, in either the one-party system or the two-party system, argues Sithole. "It is not the form but the content that counts, and that content is the will of the majority."

Madeira Keita makes the same point. "Democracy is the management of public interests in accordance with the will of the masses, the will of the greatest number. But while we want to clean up the situation, to deprive the colonialists or the adversaries of the weapon of division . . . it must nevertheless be recognised that the system of a single party is not without its dangers."

These dangers, in fact, cannot be underestimated, as events in Africa in the past two years have shown only too well. Failure to recognise these dangers springs primarily from a failure to appreciate that political parties are expressions of class realities, and that in Africa, despite certain differences compared with other regions of the world, classes are in a process of formation and different class interests exist. While accepting the mobility of classes in Africa it would be illusory to draw the conclusion that therefore class conflicts are of no significance. Madeira Keita admits that "we obviously cannot assert that Negro African society is a classless society", but he nevertheless claims that "the differentiation of classes in Africa does not imply a diversification of interests and still less an opposition of interests".

A Party for the Working Class

This is broadly true in so far as the struggle against colonialism is concerned, but as the struggle to reconstruct the economy unfolds and the battle is joined for a better life, for fundamental land reform, and for decision whether the path of development should be a capitalist one or not, divergence of class interests and class views is bound to grow.

Julius Nyerere has said:

"In the future it is possible that a second political party will grow in Tanganyika, but in one sense such a growth would represent a failure by T.A.N.U. The existence of two or more stable political parties implies a class structure of society, and we aim at avoiding the growth of social and economic classes in our country. If we do avoid this, then opposition will take the form of disagreement on how to do things which we agree should be done. It is not essential that this type of disagreement be expressed through a two-party system."

The implication of this argument is that at present there are no divergent classes in Tanganyika and that the stage of class society can somehow be avoided in the future. It is true that there is no rich powerful feudal landowning class in Tanganyika, nor a flourishing national bourgeoisie; the African employers of labour are numerically small and economically not a powerful force. Yet even here classes are developing, and if Tanganyika is to evolve into a classless form of society then it must by-pass the full capitalist stage of development and first construct socialist society as the preliminary step towards the classless society of communism. But to accomplish this the working class cannot confine itself to being a subordinate force in a single mass party whose ideology and leading personnel include other classes and other views. The construction of socialism requires that the working class assume a leading position, either within the single mass party or through separate organisation. It is only in this way that the working people can be led to power and the building of socialism.

This need is becoming recognised in Africa.

"The political parties that have unfurled the banner of socialism must quickly and decisively convert themselves from nationalist mass movements into armies of dedicated militants of socialism. Only such far-reaching changes within these political parties will facilitate the transmission of socialist ideas to the masses, more especially to the workers, peasants and youths. . . . Simultaneously, the new political parties must enable the best elements from within the rank and file of the workers and peasants to become an integral part of Africa's new political leadership."

(*The Spark:* Accra, 29 December 1962.)

This argument applies in general to all African states; and in all of them the path following the winning of political independence is certain to be one of difficulty and class conflict, even though the conflict may vary considerably in intensity. Describing this new stage Khrushchov has pointed out:

"The countries freed from colonial oppression have entered a new phase of development. The struggle for political independence united all the national forces that suffered under the colonialists and shared common interests. Now that the time has come to eradicate the roots of imperialism and introduce agrarian and other urgent social reforms, the differences in class interests are coming more and more into the open. Broad sections of the working people and also that

considerable section of the national bourgeoisie which is
interested in the accomplishment of the basic tasks of the
anti-imperialist, anti-feudal revolution, want to go farther to
strengthen independence and carry out social and economic
reforms. Within the ruling circles of those countries, however,
there are forces that are afraid to go farther in their collaboration with the democratic, progressive section of the nation.
They would like to appropriate the fruits of the people's
struggle and hamper the further development of the national
revolution. These forces compromise with imperialism outside the country and feudalism within, and resort to dictatorial
methods."

(N. S. Khrushchov: Report of the Central Committee of the
C.P.S.U. to the 22nd Congress, 17 October 1961.)

The reality of this class conflict is amply demonstrated by the
experience of Egypt. Here dominant sections of the national
bourgeoisie, a relatively powerful monopoly class, have taken
supreme power into their hands and installed a terrorist form of
dictatorship over the workers and peasants in the form of the
suppression of all democratic organisations and parties and the
overall domination of a single party or organisation, the National
Union. In these circumstances, the one-party system, far from
being a form for uniting the whole people against colonialism
and its remnants, has become a means for the suppression of one
part of the people, the majority, by another part, the capitalist
minority. This has deepened the divisions between the people
and weakened the very national unity in whose name the dictatorship has falsely been established. This shows only too well how
the one-party system can be a source of danger to the people of
Africa, a means by which the national bourgeoisie can suppress
the workers, peasants and democratic intelligentsia.

Similarly, in the Brazzaville group of former French colonies
in Africa one can see how this one-party system has, in many
cases, come into being on the basis of suppressing the genuinely
democratic organisations, both trade union and political, in the
interests of a ruling group who wish to appropriate the fruits of
independence for themselves.

It is clear that in those African states where the working class
is excluded from all influence in the state, where imperialist

puppets or reactionary local capitalists rule, the one-party system is a threat to the people and a means of holding them down. In other African states, such as Guinea, Ghana and Mali, where patriotic democrats play a leading role, where the working class exercises considerable influence and where the national bourgeoisie is either weak or does not enjoy undivided dominion over the state and the economy, the one-party state may, under certain conditions, make possible the growth of working-class influence and of Marxist-Leninist ideology within the single party to the stage where these forces enjoy majority support and thus make possible a special form of development.

In this connection it is not without interest that when members of the Mongolian People's Revolutionary Party visited Lenin in 1921 they discussed with him the question of turning the party into a Communist Party, and asked his opinion. Lenin expressed the view that there was still much to do in building up the new state and in developing the country's economy and culture before an adequate working-class force could be created from amongst the herdsmen, a force which, in due time, would help develop the People's Revolutionary Party into a fully Marxist party. It would be harmful and dangerous, he thought, to simply change the signboard.

As long as it is possible for the working class to play an effective part in the mass national party, to defend its class interests, to put forward its own ideas concerning all aspects of national development, to study, discuss and propagate Marxist concepts, then the maintenance of the single mass party and its progressive development into a party clearly based on scientific socialism will be possible.

If, however, the working class finds its activities limited within the single party, if the newly developing capitalist forces assume dictatorial control of the party and strive to turn the whole direction of the nation on to a capitalist path, then it is inevitable that the working class will seek to establish its own political party which can defend its own class interests and, at the same time, uphold the deepest interests of the nation as a whole.

Further than that, it can indeed be said that both the needs of full national development, as well as that of the fullest flowering of democracy, require that the working class should be allowed its full political rights as a class, up to and including the right to set up its own political party. But a working-class party, if it is to fully express the outlook and aspirations of its class and to lead the whole nation, must be based on scientific socialist ideas, on the philosophy of Marxism-Leninism. It is a regrettable fact that in many African states which have won their political independence, the undemocratic suppression of scientific socialist ideas and of Marxist-Leninist organisations, which was a hall-mark of the colonial system, is carried on by some of the new African governments, very often at the direct bidding of the imperialists themselves. And in acting thus, these governments use the same arguments as those of the imperialists—the arguments of "anti-communism", the pretence that communism is against democracy and that it is a means by which Russia will gain control of Africa.

But it is the communists—those in the Soviet Union and other socialist states, those in Britain, those in Africa—who are the most consistent champions of Africa's fight for independence and democracy, for the democratic right of the African people to have their own governments and rule their countries, for the democratic franchise of "one man, one vote", for the democratic ownership and control of African resources by African people, for the fullest democratic power in the hands of the working people, the workers, peasants, intellectuals, artisans and others, so that they can plan their own future and use the wealth of their countries in their own interests. No communist, neither in the Soviet Union nor in Africa, wants to see any Russians ruling in Africa. It is Africans who must rule Africa. It is the enemies of Africa, the imperialists, those who yesterday arbitrarily ruled over Africa and who today dream of maintaining that rule by the methods of neo-colonialism, who fear the communists and who, to keep their grip on Africa, spread these false ideas about the communists. Every fighter for African independence knows how the imperialists stick the label "communist" on national leaders. That is what reactionary American politicians called Nkrumah; that is what Sir Edgar Whitehead called Nkomo. The imperialists hope that in this way the African people will be scared away from anti-imperialists. In fact, however, this communist-phobia of the imperialists is a measure of the important role which the communists and the ideas of Marxism-Leninism can play in completing the tasks of national liberation and advancing to socialism.

It is significant that in Indonesia, where the government of the national bourgeoisie, led by President Sukarno, works in close alliance with the Indonesian Communist Party, and where the people have recently won a signal victory in securing the retreat of the Dutch imperialists from West Irian, President Sukarno himself should regard the elimination of these false phobias about the communists as one of the most significant developments in Indonesia. In his speech to the closing rally of the National Congress of the Indonesian Communist Party, on 30 April 1962, he said that formerly "a part of the Indonesian people regarded the communists as the very devil incarnate on this earth". He found this "disturbing", since he knew that "the communists are well-intentioned, and especially in our struggle to smash imperialism, the contribution the communists have made has not been a small one". But things in Indonesia are different now, and Sukarno declares his considerable satisfaction in having "succeeded in cleansing communist-phobia from the hearts of the majority of the people". Further, says Sukarno, if you agree with democracy, you must include the communists, who are an essential part of the people; if you believe in national unity, you must include the communists for the same reason; and if you believe in mobilising the people for struggle, again you must include the communists.

These remarks of President Sukarno are equally applicable to Africa. Anti-communism, "communist-phobia", the suppression of Marxism-Leninism as a system of thought, the attempt to crush communist organisations—all this is not only a limitation on democracy in Africa. It is no less a limitation on national development, a weakening of the national cause, of the truest interests of the mass of the people, and an assistance to the imperialists. A long line of tyrants—Thiers, Tsar Nicholas II, Mannerheim, Mussolini, Hitler, Franco, Chiang Kai-shek, Syngman Rhee, Diem, McCarthy, Salazar, Verwoerd, Welensky, Batista, Jimenez, Trujillo and many more—based their dictatorships on anti-communism. It is regrettable that some African leaders have picked up this tattered mantle of the dictators and imperialists.

The Opposition in Ghana

Ghana, as mentioned above, is often singled out when questions of democracy in Africa are discussed. Critics of Ghana usually ignore class realities; even liberal sympathisers with Ghana's national and democratic cause often judge Ghana on the basis of the form in which things are done, not on the content. Thus, because the Ghana Government has found it necessary to take stern measures against its opponents, some people argue that it is therefore acting undemocratically. Yet, when the British Government rounded up Mosley and his fascists during the war and put them in jail under 18B, without trial, the British people fully understood that this "undemocratic" action was essential for the defence of real democracy. In fact, many thought the government too lenient.

But the people of countries such as Ghana, having just secured political independence after years of bitter struggle, and now facing the hostile forces of imperialism which are striving by every possible means to thwart or overturn the verdict of history, have an equally tense situation to face, and are surely justified in taking strong action to defend their new state. This has been a law practised by all revolutionary states, by the Cromwellian Revolution which executed a king, by the great French Revolution, by the Russian Revolution of October 1917, the Chinese Liberation of 1949 and the Cuban Revolution of 1959.

Equally all great revolutions and movements for national liberation have been confronted, on the morrow of their victory, with frantic struggle, subversion and assassination on the part of the forces of reaction. Was not Abraham Lincoln assassinated? Was not a similar attempt made on the life of Lenin? Were not Aung Sang and many other Burmese leaders murdered on the dawn of their victory? Did not Gandhi in India and Bandaranaike in Ceylon suffer the same fate? Have there not been several attempts on the life of Sukarno, of Sekou Toure and of other national leaders? And, above all, have we not the experience of the overthrow of the democratic government of Guatemala, the American-sponsored attack on Cuba, and martyred Congo, with its great leader Lumumba brutally killed within the first few months of that country's formal independence?

There really should be little doubt that the "Opposition" to the Ghana Government represents the forces of the past, an alliance of disgruntled capitalist politicians, tribal reactionaries, and ambitious officers, backed by external imperialist finance and support. The Ghana Government's White Paper (*Statement by the Government on the Recent Conspiracy:* Accra, 11 December 1961) correctly explains:

> "Colonialism was responsible for producing a small re-actionary Ghanaian 'élite' drawn from the professional classes and the agents and senior employees of the great merchant houses and educated to look at every social problem from an essentially colonial standpoint. They hoped on Independence to step into the shoes of the former colonial rulers but they had no intention of altering the social system which they hoped to inherit."

This élite, explains the White Paper, was able to exploit tribal differences in Ghana which were themselves the product of colonial rule; and they allied themselves with a section of self-seekers who had worked their way into important positions in the governmental machine. It was this grouping which launched the unprincipled attack on the government towards the end of 1961 with the aim of overthrowing it and dragging the country back into complete dependence on imperialism. Those who might have been sceptical about the Ghana Government's case at the time can have little cause to doubt now, for Dr. Busia and his confederates have thrown all caution to the winds and have openly revealed themselves as plotting, in alliance with foreign imperialism, to overthrow the present Ghana Government under the leadership of President Nkrumah. A dispatch from Hella Pick (*Guardian:* 1 February 1962) makes this perfectly clear:

> "Far from hiding in fear of the long arm of Dr. Nkrumah's vengeance, Dr. Kofi Busia, Ghana's exiled Opposition leader, was to be found today in a Lagos hotel, planning an alternative government in Ghana and talking with President Olympio of Togoland and with Senegal's Foreign Minister. . . . He [Dr. Busia] is busy travelling and organising opposition groups in

Togo and the Ivory Coast where there are sizeable Ghanaian populations in favour of a change of government in Ghana. He now has an agent enlisting money and other support in the United States. . . . Dr. Busia clearly appeared to be in touch with Mr. Gbedemah, Ghana's former Minister of Finance. . . . Plans are clearly being hatched. . . ."

And the plans are to overthrow, with foreign help, the democratically elected government of Ghana. Yet when the Ghana Government takes the necessary steps to remove such threats to the democratic verdict of the people, the capitalist press in the west, with the misguided support of muddled liberals, howls in rage not against these neo-colonialist agents who threaten democracy but against the democratically elected government!

It must be admitted that one of the reasons why some people have been so confused is that amongst those arrested were a handful of trade unionists. But this in itself does not change the nature of the conspiracy against the Ghana Government. Some misguided workers took part in the Kronstadt revolt against the young Soviet power in 1921, but Lenin showed no hesitation in taking the necessary firm steps to crush the revolt, pointing out that working-class participation did not change the character of the revolt itself. The question was, he stressed, "Whose interests does it serve?" And it was clear that the enemies of working-class power were behind the revolt, and that it was their interests which were being served by this action. Similarly, during the attempt to overthrow the people's power in Hungary in October 1956 some misguided workers were used by the forces of international and internal reaction, and a number of them participated in strikes which in that situation could only help the fascists. More recently we have seen American dollars used to stir up demonstrations and strikes in British Guiana against the elected Progressive People's Party government led by Dr. Cheddi Jagan.

The strike organised in Ghana in September 1961 served similar reactionary ends. Even though some misguided workers took part in it—and there may have well been some resentment over certain aspects of the Budget—there is ample evidence (see the Ghana Government White Paper) confirming that those who actually organised the strike were in close touch with Dr. Busia and those plotting to overthrow the government. The sympathy shown by the British capitalist press towards the strikers should be sufficient to convince all but the most politically unsophisticated that no genuine working-class interests were being served by the strike.

No one would deny that the strong powers in the hands of the Ghana Government and state, which have been used to quell the anti-government conspiracy, could also be used against the working people; and naturally the Ghanaian workers and peasants will remain vigilant to prevent such a thing happening.

The maintenance and constant expansion of democracy in Ghana, as in other forward-looking African states, depends on the people helping to keep their government facing in a generally forward direction, to assist all the government's measures which are progressive, and, where there are aspects of policy which might be detrimental to the people's interests, to carry on constructive criticism, through the trade union, political and other organisations with the aim of removing the difficulty and not from the standpoint of a negative attitude towards the government, least of all by becoming a catspaw for reaction and outside intervention. If, through the process of time and the development of certain unfavourable factors, a minority anti-people's dictatorship were to emerge, then of course the people would have to take the necessary steps to overthrow such a dictatorship. This, in fact, is the viewpoint of the present Ghana Government which declares, in its White Paper, that its view does not "exclude the necessity of peoples who are oppressed having, on occasion, to overthrow a tyrannical government by force".

In the last resort the further democratic development of the new African states depends on the extent to which the people, the workers and peasants in particular, enjoy the facilities for the utmost expression of their demands, and on the possibilities for the working class being able to organise itself as a class even to the extent of forming its own working-class party.

CHAPTER FIVE

PAN-AFRICANISM AND
"AFRICAN PERSONALITY"

For many people in Europe, the term "Pan-Africanism" conjures up visions of other "pan" movements—Pan-Germanism, Pan-Slavism and so on—which played a reactionary role in history. But Pan-Africanism cannot be considered in the same light. It arose as an expression of the struggle of oppressed peoples against racial discrimination and for more than sixty years has been a feature of Africa's struggle for independence.

In its origins the Pan-African movement embraced all of Negro descent and was not confined to Africa. In fact, its earliest proponents were from the West Indies or from the United States of America. The very term "Pan-African" was originally used by a Trinidad lawyer, William Sylvester, at the first Pan-African Conference held in London in 1900. And at this conference the American Negro scholar, Dr. W. E. B. Du Bois, who for generations has taught and inspired scores of Africa's present leaders, played an important role. Efforts continued for more than a decade to build up support for the Pan-African movement, which acquired a new impetus from the experiences of the first world war, and the events which followed it. Hundreds of thousands of Africans took part in this war "to save democracy" and "to end all wars". They fought on battlefields in Europe as well as in Africa, and in the course of these actions they began to acquire a deeper understanding of the nature of imperialism and of their own destiny as a people. There was considerable feeling in Africa that the first world war was "a white man's war" in which the interests of the African people were not involved. Partly arising from this feeling, and partly from the difficult economic and social conditions which the war had given rise to, protest movements and revolts took place in a number of territories. There was rioting in Liberia, revolts in Dahomey, a widespread movement in Kenya, and an uprising in Nyasaland, led by John Chilembwe, aimed, in part, against African participation in the war. Something of the feeling and viewpoint of the African people towards the war is captured by Chilembwe in his important document *The Voice of African Natives in the Present War*, written towards the end of 1914, shortly after a skirmish between "German" and "British" forces in East Africa in which five-sixths of the casualties on both sides were African. Chilembwe protested that "the poor Africans who have nothing to own in this present world, who in death leave only a long line of widows and orphans in utter want and dire distress, are invited to die for a cause which is not theirs".

But the spirit of revolt shown in the Nyasaland rising was no isolated affair. As Lewis Garnett Jordan, a leading American Baptist, explained eloquently:

"With 600,000 Africans fighting in the trenches with the allies and an equal number in arms in various parts of Africa under governments who have taken over the continent, it can never be hoped to again make the African a docile creature, to be driven like a dumb brute, which his oppressors have been 100 years or more in the making."
(*Pebbles from an African Beach:* Philadelphia, 1918.)

Events were to prove him right. The experiences of the war and the impact of the 1917 October Revolution in Russia had a significant effect on the people of Africa. This was indicated, for instance, by the complaints of Gold Coast missionaries that African soldiers returning after 1918 showed "communistic" tendencies. The early post-1918 years witnessed, too, the birth of the West African National Congress (1920), the Industrial and Commercial Workers' Union (1918–20), and the Communist Party of South Africa (1921), as well as the Kenya crisis of 1921.

Pan-African Congresses

The Pan-African Congress of 1919, called under the name "Pan-African" for the first time, was inspired by the same influences and forces which had given rise to the above events. Between 1919 and 1945 five Pan-African Congresses were held—in Paris, London and Brussels, Lisbon, New York and Manchester. Not until 1958, after Ghana had become independent, was it to be possible to hold such a conference on African soil. Owing to the conditions under which these Congresses were held, direct, living contact with the people and their struggles in Africa was not always possible; partly in consequence of this delegates were to some extent American Negroes; sometimes West Indians; and the Africans were usually students or temporary exiles from their native lands. Yet it would be wrong to regard these conferences as completely unrepresentative. They were, in a general way, the voice and conscience of Africa; and, increasingly, from conference to conference, they became the thinking advance-guard of the African peoples' independence movements, many of their adopted policies, concepts and declarations anticipating, by a number of years, the programmes of African national organisations which developed after the second world war, and containing, too, many of the fundamental principles which have since been proclaimed by the All-African Peoples Conference. In addition, a number of delegates to the Pan-African Congresses later returned home to become leaders of the national movements which, in many cases, they initiated. Amongst such leaders who were partly reared by the Pan-African Congress movement were Jomo Kenyatta, Dr. Kwame Nkrumah, Dr. Azikiwe and Dr. Hastings Banda.

To gain an understanding of the main ideas developed and put forward by the Pan-African Congress movement it is necessary to examine their decisions and resolutions. The First Pan-African Congress, held in Paris in 1919 and attended by fifty-seven delegates, adopted a resolution which, amongst other things, demanded the right of Africans to participate in government, commencing with local and tribal government, and being gradually extended "to the higher offices of state; to the end that, in time, Africa is ruled by consent of the Africans". Thus, at an early date, the principle of full political rights for Africans was adopted, though at this stage it was seen as an eventual achievement rather than as an immediate demand; and, moreover, the conception of national independence and of political power in the hands of the African people was not yet clearly formulated.

The Second Congress was held in 1921, in London and Brussels, and there were 113 delegates present, including forty-one from Africa. The Congress adopted a "Declaration to the World" which called for the "establishment of political institutions among suppressed peoples", and demanded "local self-government for backward groups" leading to "complete self-government". The Third Congress, held in Lisbon and London in 1923, also went no further than the two previous ones in regard to the question of government, limiting its demand to that of a voice for Africans in their governments. At the same time there was emphasis that the development of Africa should take place for the Africans and not merely for the profit of Europeans. The Fourth Congress, which was held in New York in 1927, did not really carry the movement very much further forward.

It was not until 1945, when the Fifth Congress was held, that one could see a really decisive change. The experience of the war, the defeat of fascism and the rise of the new socialist states, resulted in a fundamental change in the balance of forces in the world which found expression, too, in the internal developments within the different countries. Everywhere the people were on the march; trade unions were formed and grew, women and young people set up organisations, greater use was made of democratic rights, the struggle for national independence in Asia and Africa mounted to new heights and won new victories. Historically speaking, the world had "moved Left", had heeled over away from imperialism and reaction and in the direction of national independence, democracy and socialism.

The same tide of change swept over Africa, and found significant expression at the Fifth Pan-African Congress held in Manchester in October 1945. The previous Pan-African Congresses, despite the efforts of their organisers, had been mainly gatherings of intellectuals. But by the end of the second world war the world had been so transformed and the movements

in Africa had made such progress that it was the mass organisations, the national parties and the trade unions in particular,
that were the dominant influence at the Fifth Pan-African
Congress.

The resolutions adopted by the Congress reflected the change
no less than did the basis of representation. Demanding independence for the African people, its Declaration to the Colonial
Peoples stated, in unequivocal terms:

> "We affirm the right of all colonial peoples to control their
> own destiny. All colonies must be free from foreign imperialist
> control, whether political or economic.
>
> The peoples of the colonies must have the right to elect
> their own governments, without restrictions from foreign
> powers. We say to the peoples of the colonies that they must
> fight for these ends by all means at their disposal.
>
> The object of the imperialist powers is to exploit. By granting
> the right of colonial peoples to govern themselves that object
> is defeated. Therefore, the struggle for political power by
> colonial and subject peoples is the first step towards, and the
> necessary prerequisite to, complete social, economic and
> political emancipation. . . . Colonial workers must be in the
> front of the battle against imperialism. . . . Today there is
> only one road to effective action—the organisation of the
> masses. . . . Colonial and subject peoples of the world, Unite!"

One cannot help but notice the difference not only in tone but
also in the character and preciseness of the demands of the 1945
Congress in comparison with those of the earlier Congresses.
The 1945 Congress was clearly an anti-colonial Congress, international in spirit, and influenced by socialist thought no less
than the experience of anti-imperialist struggle.

Within the next few years the scene of interest shifted from
Pan-Africanist Congresses in Europe, to the actual organisation
of the struggle in Africa, a struggle in which a number of the
leading figures were those who had been prominent at the 1945
Congress.

The birth of Ghana in March 1957 gave a new impetus to the
Pan-African movement, and provided new opportunities for its
growth. Independent Ghana became, as it were, the new base

from which the ideas of Pan-Africanism could spread, and it was therefore natural that the first conference of Independent African States was held at Accra, 15–22 April 1958, and the first All-African Peoples Conference, also at Accra, in December 1958. Eight independent African states—Ghana, Liberia, Ethiopia, Libya, Sudan, Morocco, Tunisia and the United Arab Republic —attended the first conference of African States, whose deliberations were clearly inspired by the ideas of the Pan-African movement.

The Principles of Pan-Africanism

It would, perhaps, be useful if, at this point, we considered the ideology of Pan-Africanism.

Pan-Africanism is based on four main principles. First, that the people of the entire African continent have a common destiny and therefore need to unite their efforts to the utmost in order to solve their problems. Secondly, that Africa must be ruled by Africans and that all forms of foreign domination and influence, all forms and manifestations of colonialism, must be swept away. Thirdly, that to achieve unity and to destroy colonialism, the African people must re-establish their own history, revive the memory of their own national heroes and struggles for freedom, rekindle their own languages and culture, reassert their own dignity and recognise that they have their own distinct contribution to make to the progress of human society; these ideas go to make up the conception of the "African personality". Fourthly, that, following the ending of direct colonial rule, African society must be radically reorganised—economically, socially and politically. In short, Pan-Africanism is African independence, African unity, "African personality" and radical social change— and all four conceptions are closely linked.

These principles of Pan-Africanism, which have developed over the years in the course of the struggles of the African peoples, through the thinking of their leaders, the deliberations of the Pan-African Congresses, and the activities of the African people's organisations, were summed up in the stirring words which dominated the platform at the First All-African Peoples Conference in December 1958:

"Peoples of Africa unite
We have nothing to lose but our chains
We have a continent to regain
We have freedom and human dignity to attain"

These conceptions were equally voiced by the different speakers at the First Conference of Independent African States. Kwame Nkrumah, in particular, who has been the most consistent and energetic champion of Pan-Africanism, made special reference to the question of African unity and to the need for the African people to express their own African personality.

"Although this was the first time that most of the representatives of the Independent African States had met each other, we soon discovered that on all matters of vital importance to our respective countries, we all had a common community of interests which has been strikingly reflected in our resolutions and decisions. . . . We were most agreeably surprised by the singular 'one-ness' which unfolded itself as speaker after speaker made his contribution to our discussions. . . . We are one, an entity symbolised by our united African Personality. . . . The community of aim and purpose expressed by our African Personality will allow us in the future to play a *positive role* and speak with a concerted voice in the cause of Peace, and for the liberation of dependent Africa and in defence of our national independence, sovereignty and territorial integrity."

No one at all familiar with the history of Africa can fail to appreciate and sympathise with the African people's desire to stand on their own feet, to slough off every vestige of colonialism in outlook, culture and behaviour. For over four centuries they knew slavery, the lash and the sword, the robbery of their land and resources, the break-up of their families, the carving up of their territory and the arbitrary and ruthless tearing up of ethnic groups. African languages were ignored by the colonial authorities and the languages of the conquerors—English, French, Portuguese, Spanish, German, Italian—were made "official". These were the languages taught in schools, spoken in court, used in edicts. As with languages, so with culture. The African people's own culture, still often admittedly in process of formation yet already rich in tradition and with its own distinctive contributions to make to the common culture of the world, was set aside, scorned and even denied. African history suffered the same fate at the hands of colonialism. The European rulers claimed that Africa "had no history", no past and no achievements. In the schools—themselves catering for but a handful—the African children were taught European history; they learnt about English kings and queens or French emperors, but nothing about their own destinies. Cecil Rhodes, Stanley, Marshal Lyautey—these were the "heroes" whom African people were asked to respect. Even the names of territories and towns and lakes—Rhodesia, Stanleyville, Leopoldville, Salisbury, Port Elizabeth, Pietermaritzburg, Novo Lisboa, Lake Victoria—honoured European rulers and adventurers and in other ways recalled European associations, as if there were no African place names available. And in the towns, statues of imperialist conquerors stood as if to taunt the African people with an ever-present reminder of their subject status.

Everything conceivable was done by the imperialists to stamp out from the minds of the African people the memory of their own characteristics or attainments, to instil in them the belief that they were "inferior" people, without a past, without culture, without language and with nothing to their credit. In this way, hoped the imperialists, the African people would assume doubts in their own capacities, would grow more humble, more easily accept their heavy yoke and do nothing to change things. Above all else, the colonial authorities strove to prevent the African people getting to know of their own past struggles against oppression, against slavery, against foreign conquest, against the effects of imperialist rule, against the whole colonial system. The names of African heroes were "taboo", or dismissed as "agitators", and even as "madmen". When African leaders tried to set up their own schools to teach their children the real history of their countries and to explain to them what were their rights—as Chilembwe tried to do in Nyasaland and Kenyatta in Kenya—then the full wrath of the government came down, and the schools were suppressed.

Added to all this was the shameful practice of racial discrimination which ate into the heart of society right across the continent. This foul pestilence laid its hands on everything. Because of their colour Africans were not allowed to use the same shops, the same restaurants, the same cinemas, swimming baths (sometimes even bathing beaches), park seats, buses, trains, post-offices, lavatories and churches, even whole districts and sometimes towns, as the European. They were debarred from higher education and from certain hospitals. They were denied access to certain jobs and professions, kept in the most menial employ, and even where they obtained better jobs were paid a tithe of the European wage or salary. The greater the number of white settlers, the worse the discrimination. So much for the European civilising mission to "uplift" the "heathen"! It is a striking commentary on European rule that it is precisely where European settlement was less, such as Ghana, Nigeria, Sierra Leone, that educational advance amongst Africans was most rapid; and, conversely, where European settlement was heavy, as in the Congo, Angola, Mozambique, the Rhodesias, Kenya, that a mere handful of Africans were able to secure university training.

Is it really any wonder if, in the face of all this, the African people at last cried out: "Enough! We are not inferior peoples, nor are we going to let you keep us in a subordinate position any longer. And what is more, we are determined, from now on, to express our own personality, to have our own thoughts, develop our own ideas and policies, based on our own African soil, our own African circumstances, our own history, our own struggles, traditions, languages, culture and achievements."

"*African Personality*"

Ndabaningi Sithole, a leader of the national movement in Southern Rhodesia, has defined the term "African personality" in these words:

"This personality finds satisfaction in African politics, economics, education, art, culture and a host of other things. This means that African politics can never be the same thing as European or American politics. European or American systems can never be those of Africa. . . . The idea of *African personality* can be gleaned in the movement of Pan-Africanism

—the excessive desire on the part of the African people to be and to remain themselves in opposition to being converted into black Englishmen, Frenchmen and Portuguese—and in that of African nationalism—the Africans' excessive desire to control their own destiny rather than to have it controlled by outsiders."

(*The Voice of Africa*: August 1961.)

Or, as put by Kwame Nkrumah, "The African must assert his own personality and develop according to his own ways of life, his own customs, traditions and culture."

In illustration of this concept of the African personality Sithole shows how it expresses itself politically, economically, in culture and education, and in military questions.

Politically, he says, it expresses itself in its "strong rejection of white domination in Africa, in its determination to destroy that domination, root, stem and branch". Therefore, it aims at complete independence, at "total emancipation from foreign rule" and at being "master of its own destiny in Africa". The African personality, he writes, "died with political dependence, but rose from the dead with political independence. . . . The army of Europeans who spoke for Africans has been pushed aside. Africa now speaks for herself. She does not have to act as a carbon copy for European ideas, thoughts, actions. She does not have to perform the role of rubber-stamping European schemes and plans."

On the economic level, stresses Sithole, the African is mindful of his past status under which the European powers regarded Africa "as a source of human and raw materials. The human beings of Africa were viewed in the light of economic exploitation. . . . Second, Africa was regarded as dumping ground for the finished goods of Europe." In consequence of this policy of imperialism, the African was "dehumanised, depersonalised, devalued", and his human dignity insulted and besmirched by his being treated simply "as an economic tool", his initiative and genius crippled and frustrated. Now all this is changing. The African is no longer the passive consumer or performer of European economic plans. "He has ceased to be a means to European ends. He now exists in his own right. He is an end in himself in his economic sphere." This is expressed in Africa's strong opposition to joining the European Common Market and in its desire to form an African Common Market.

Culturally, African songs, dances, dress, customs and traditions, which suffered such a set-back under the colonial system, "have suddenly sprung to life as a result of political independence". African music, painting, sculpture, dancing, even opera, a new form for Africa, is suddenly flourishing. African research is rediscovering Africa's past and her heroes brought out into the sun of the people's acclamation. "The entire continent", says Sithole, "seems to be throbbing and pulsating with things African. . . . They seem to be shouting with one big voice: 'Give me back my Africa, and the things that are African!' "

In education there is the same development. The entire consciousness of the African students, as Sithole points out, "was thoroughly immersed with white heroes and black villains". The colonialist strove to destroy the African personality in every classroom. There was even a distinction made with the teachers. European teachers were called "Mr. So-and-so", whereas African teachers went by the name of "Teacher So-and-so". But now African education is undergoing a complete overhaul. "The African-personality-killing school books are being rewritten or discarded altogether." African schools no longer teach white supremacy, but the equality of all men.

From a military standpoint, too, African people feel that their personality was crushed under colonialism, and that in this sphere, no less than in others, fundamental changes must be made. During the first and second world wars, as we have already noted, the imperialists appealed to the Africans to provide soldiers for the defence of "freedom and democracy". But when the fighting and the dying was over, the African people found that in the very land of their birth they were denied the things for which they had allegedly been fighting. Once again they found themselves "cheated, cajoled, duped by the imperialists". Once again they had been "used" by imperialism, this time as military weapons; once again they discovered that the imperialists used them simply as instruments to serve colonialist ends, but never considered them as people. From now on, however, the African is determined that he and his land will no longer be used for foreign military purposes. Africa will be no foreign military base, will sign no military pacts linking it with interests other than its own and will not fight for any cause not in Africa's interests. Today, in fact, "African soldiers . . . train to defend African freedom, not European freedom".

Similarly in the field of law, all African customary law was cast aside, and European legal systems, based on capitalist conceptions of private property, introduced. Africa is now evolving its own legal systems, based on tradition and on the requirements of the newly developing African states. European parliamentary systems, too, are being rejected, as we have already seen. Even in the trade union sphere the attempt by the imperialists to set up tame trade unions, which would actually help to maintain the colonial system, has broken down; and the formation of the All-African Trade Union Federation is an expression of the determination of African workers to have their own, independent trade union, severed from all connections with imperialism and neo-colonialism, or its agents of the I.C.F.T.U.

Thus in every sphere of human endeavour Africa is now staunchly expressing its own personality and defending its own interests. In short, despite the struggles which still lie ahead to end direct colonial rule in many parts of Africa and to defeat the new threats of neo-colonialism, Africa today, in the words of Ndabaningi Sithole, is "the captain of her soul, and master of her own destiny".

Imperialism and its agents try to turn this just and historically inevitable desire of the African people to speak—in Nkrumah's words—"through the voices of Africa's own sons", into a source of confusion and disruption, and as a means of stirring up racial strife. Thus, those who for centuries preached and practised the most vile forms of racialism, of white supremacy, now turn round and declare that expressing the African personality means creating a form of African chauvinism. All the voices of the African organisations and leading political figures give the lie to this argument. Nkrumah has emphasised:

"Our emphasis upon Africa bespeaks neither chauvinism nor isolationism. . . . We welcome men of good will everywhere to join us, irrespective of their race, religion, or nationality. When I speak of Africa for Africans, this should be interpreted in the light of my emphatic declaration that I do not believe in racialism and colonialism. The concept 'Africa

for the Africans' does not mean that other races are excluded from it. It only means that Africans, who naturally are in the majority in Africa, shall and must govern themselves in their own countries. The fight is for the future of humanity. . . ."
(*Voice of Africa:* October 1961.)

Similarly the heroic Patrice Lumumba once emphasised:
"Our movement does not rebel against the white people. We have only one enemy—colonialism—and not the European people."

Kenneth Kaunda, too, the leader of the United National Independence Party of Northern Rhodesia, has explained that the cry of "Africa for the Africans" was "no more than the legitimate cry for majority rule. . . . Time and again we have said what we still say now, that those Europeans who are willing to work in peace and harmony under a democratically elected African government are more than welcome here." Ruben Um Nyobe, great son of the Kamerunian people, who was murdered by French troops in 1958, voiced the true internationalism of the African liberation movement when he wrote:

"[we] do not confuse the British people with British imperialism which holds people under its sway, nor the French people with the French colonialists who pillage and oppress the people of our country. We must warn our brothers against the dangers involved in a policy of hate against the White Man. Racial hatred is incompatible with any idea of progress."
(*The Immediate Unification of Kamerun:* 1951.)

How noble and generous are the voices of Nkrumah, Lumumba, Kaunda and Nyobe beside the strident, panic-stricken, hate-filled shrieks of the Tory backwoodsmen, the Welenskys and Verwoerds, the French, Belgian and Portuguese colons, the American racialists of Little Rock and Washington!

Distortions of Pan-Africanism

What often causes confusion is that the slogan "Pan-Africanism" is sometimes used by those who distort its meaning to suit their own narrow purposes. Thus, in the Republic of South Africa, there is the so-called "Pan-Africanist Congress" or P.A.C., which has usurped the title "Pan-Africanist", though its policy runs counter to nearly all the positive historical demands and policies of the Pan-Africanist movement.

Thus, outstanding leaders of the genuine Pan-African movement, such as Nkrumah, Lumumba, Kaunda, Nyobe, as we have just seen, have warned against the dangers involved in anti-white chauvinism. But the P.A.C. is based on chauvinism, and refuses to co-operate with the African National Congress on the grounds that this body works with progressive Coloured people, Indians and Europeans.

A further tenet of the Pan-African movement is the unity of the peoples against imperialism, colonialism and neo-colonialism. The P.A.C. is not only against such unity in words, but in deeds it has constantly sabotaged the efforts of the people to struggle against the Verwoerd government, going so far as to issue, in conjunction with the police, leaflets calling on the workers to blackleg the general strike which the A.N.C. and others had organised in protest against the government's fascist measures.

Pan-Africanism is one of the inspirations behind the formation of the All-African Trade Union Federation, which has called on all its affiliates to break with the I.C.F.T.U. Taking part in the All-African Trade Union Federation is the South African Congress of Trade Unions, open to all workers irrespective of race, and co-operating closely with the A.N.C. and other sections of the national liberation movement in South Africa. But P.A.C. leaders have openly helped to set up F.O.F.A.T.U.S.A. (the Federation of Free African Trade Unions of South Africa), a body linked with the I.C.F.T.U.

Pan-Africanism recognises the need for radical economic, social and political change in Africa; and the most advanced states are ready to co-operate with the Soviet Union and other socialist states to assist that purpose. The P.A.C., on the other hand, echoing all the slanderous propaganda of imperialism, is filled with the same violent anti-Soviet conceptions as those held by the most rabid colonialists.

The P.A.C. is not only active in South Africa, but abroad it has spread its false doctrines and tried to disrupt the national movements in several other African territories. Thus, in Angola, its collaborators attack the leaders of the Popular Movement for the Liberation of Angola (M.P.L.A.), because they are prepared to co-operate with progressive Portuguese and those of mixed Portuguese and African origin. In Zanzibar, its extreme racialism has split the movement for national independence and enabled British imperialism to maintain its power there. In Basutoland, Bechuanaland and Swaziland its agents have split the national movements by a combination of extreme racialism and anti-communism. As for the Republic of South Africa, the articles of the P.A.C. leaders devote their main energies to boosting one another and attacking such outstanding fighters against white rule as Chief Albert Luthuli and Nelson Mandela.

The P.A.C. also attacks the African National Congress because it allows communists to play a part in their organisation. But Dr. Du Bois, the father of Pan-Africanism, is himself a member of the Communist Party—and is fully entrusted by President Nkrumah with the historic task of directing the research for the publication of the *Encyclopedia Africana*. And no one can claim that Kwame Nkrumah is not faithful to the ideals of Pan-Africanism.

Imperialism is happy to see the P.A.C. act as a weapon to disrupt the African movements. But there is little doubt that African people will increasingly see through this trick.

Imperialism also seeks to turn the slogan of "African personality" to its own advantage by suggesting and encouraging ideas that would blur the sights of the African people, hide from them the class realities of the African scene and leave them without rudder or compass in the complex and difficult struggles which still lie ahead. They would like the African people to believe that the "African personality" embraces a Tshombe, a Mobutu, a Kasavubu or Ahidjoalong side Lumumba, Luthuli, Nkrumah, Sekou Toure, Keita, Kenyatta, Nyerere. They would like the African people to accept the proposition that between Tshombe and Nkrumah, simply because both are Africans, there is more in common than there is between the three staunch anti-imperialists Nkrumah, Castro and Khrushchov. The imperialists also hope that the slogan of "African personality" will make the African people forget that although they have a common interest, as Africans, in getting rid of imperialism, there is a basic difference in long-term interests and in outlook between an African capitalist and an African worker, or between an African landlord and an African peasant.

Are there Classes in Africa?

Some people are so taken up with these false interpretations of the conceptions for which the Pan-African movement stands that they have constructed a whole edifice of "African exceptionalism". Thus they have extended the concept of African personality and twisted the meaning of African history and present structure to argue that Africa has no classes: no capitalist class, no proletariat, no peasants, but just "people". The absence of classes, they argue, makes unnecessary working-class power (or the dictatorship of the proletariat) as a stage in the construction of socialism; and, moreover, because Africa has no classes, it alone, of all continents, can produce the purest form of democracy with a dictatorship neither of the bourgeoisie nor of the proletariat. Along with these conceptions is the attempt to foster a racial exclusiveness which would cut Africa off from the great national liberation movements of Asia and Latin America, and from the anti-imperialist countries which make up the socialist camp. Even the perfectly justified and, in fact, correct aim of building socialism in Africa on the basis of the specific concrete conditions, class relations and historical traditions of the African people is distorted to support a "theory" that Africa will follow "neither the capitalist road nor the communist road", but will strike out and build a different form of society, a "third social force" distinguished from both of the two main systems in the world, capitalism and socialism.

Is it true that there are no classes in Africa? People who assert that there are not, argue as if the contention that different classes exist in Africa is somehow an attempt to impose European ideas and a European pattern of society on Africa. But the existence of classes is not a European invention but a world-wide phenomenon. And when one says that there are different classes in Africa this simply means that Africa—despite its very real difference from other continents (and they, too, differ from one another)—goes through certain inevitable phases of historical development, as do all human societies. It is true, of course, that in pre-colonial Africa, although Africa had passed, in the main, beyond the stage of primitive communal society and was mainly in a stage defined by Jean Suret-Canale as "elementary feudalism", class forces were not yet fully developed and class contradictions in consequence did not become acute.

The imposition by European powers of the slave trade, apart from robbing Africa, over a period of some 400 years, of at least 50 million people, mainly the most robust, healthy and young—that is, the most direct form of the productive forces—also held back the development of the productive forces in Africa by the very nature of the slave trade itself. Slaves were exchanged for guns, gin and baubles, commodities which had no productive value. To save themselves from slavery each tribe desperately sought guns, the new powerful weapon introduced by European capitalism. But to gain guns one had to sell slaves. Hence tribe was turned against tribe, clan against clan. This internecine war, the exchange of society's main productive force, manpower, for unproductive items, prevented any advance in productive forces, any upward movement of technique, of the economy. In consequence, the conditions created by the slave trade blocked, in Africa, the normal evolution which had begun in previous societies. While in Europe, whose rulers waxed fat on the slave trade, new techniques appeared, feudalism passed into capitalism and new class forces arose, African society stagnated and froze in its primitive or elementary feudal stages.

Once Europe had passed beyond the stage of competitive capitalism and entered the stage of monopoly and imperialism, Africa underwent a further and different form of conquest, expressed in the colonial system of the twentieth century. Once more African class development was distorted. Colonialism stifled the normal growth of African productive forces. European monopoly of the mines, of trade, banking, transport and usually the best land, hindered the growth of an African capitalist class; and the exploitation of Africa as a source of cheap raw materials, accompanied by a policy of deliberate limitation of industrial production, meant a delay in the formation of a large body of permanent, semi-skilled and skilled labour, of factory workers, of a proletariat. Migrant labour, the creation of a force of peasant workers fluctuating between their own land and wage employment, became a widespread phenomenon. The survival over large parts of Africa of commonly owned land and the absence of private ownership has also influenced the pattern of class forces in Africa today.

Thus, at the time in which African territories are gaining their political independence, class forces are still in process of growth and the divisions between them not so clearly defined as in the advanced capitalist countries. It is this factor, the early stage of the formation of class forces in Africa today, the weakness of the capitalist class, the extreme mobility between workers and peasants, the somewhat limited scale, in some cases, of differentiation amongst the peasantry, and the relatively small size of the African intelligentsia, which has led some people to conclude that "there are no different classes in Africa".

Of course it would not be difficult to demonstrate that some African people sell their labour power and work for wages, some people work the land (either on communal lands or on individual plots bought or rented), some people have larger farms and employ Africans as agricultural workers, some people own shops and carry on trade, and some are owners or part-owners of enterprises employing African workers. The very existence of African trade unions shows that African workers are only too aware of their common class interests, of their identity as workers. And the steps (warmly welcomed by the people) which Kwame Nkrumah has taken to curb the business activities of Ministers and leading party figures in Ghana clearly indicates not merely the existence of an African capitalist class in Ghana, but also an attempt on its part to grow and expand its strength, confronted on the other hand by the people's endeavour to halt such a development.

The relatively limited stage of class differentiation reached in Africa is, of course, a positive factor in that it can facilitate the taking of a non-capitalist path of development. It does not guarantee that such a road will be taken, but is by no means an unimportant consideration in this respect. And it helps to explain, too, why there has been a tendency in Africa, much more so than in Asia, not only for the united people in each territory to come together to win the battle for independence but even to form one single mass party embracing the overwhelming majority of the people and expressing their aspirations and demands.

At the same time, failure to recognise that there are different classes in Africa would handicap the African organisations which are striving to reconstruct African society so as to overcome the last vestiges of colonialism. This is of special importance in the newly independent African states where, in some cases, representatives of the African national bourgeoisie are attempting to make use of their governmental positions or contacts to build up their own class economic strength and political power behind general demagogic slogans about the "national interests". It would obviously suit the purpose of these forces if they could conceal their aims by persuading the people that in Africa there are "no classes".

Recognition of class realities in modern Africa is equally important if there is to be any advance towards socialism. It is clearly to the advantage of those who wish to preserve capitalist forms in Africa—and this applies both to the imperialists as well as to local reactionary capitalist forces—if it is believed that there are no separate classes in Africa, no African capitalist class to exploit the people and no African working class which should exercise the leading role in the transition period. Many African organisations have in their programmes clauses asserting the aim of building a society without "the exploitation of man by man". To carry out such an aim clearly demands the recognition of the existence of a capitalist class whose exploiting role must be ended. Otherwise the slogan becomes an empty declamation with no meaning.

It is, perhaps, not a mere coincidence that the idea that a "classless society" already exists in Africa is being put forward at a time when, in the west, capitalist propagandists and right-wing labour leaders are claiming that classes no longer have meaning in the advanced capitalist countries. Before the war the capitalists used to pretend "we are all workers now"; but today they argue "we are all capitalists". The big imperialist monopolies which rule the west and still dominate the economics and, to a large extent, the politics, of most of Africa would like nothing better than that "this whole business of classes" could be buried and forgotten by the people. But it was recognition of class realities which made it possible for the workers and peasants of Russia, and later China and other countries in Eastern Europe and Asia, to win complete national liberation, establish the political power of the working people, and move on to the construction of socialism. It is the understanding of these same class realities in Africa, different in pattern though they may be, which will enable the African working people to move on from political independence to the formation of fully independent, democratic states and the transition to socialism.

CHAPTER SIX

TOWARDS A UNITED AFRICA

In 1885 the western imperialist powers met at the Conference of
Berlin and decided to divide up Africa amongst themselves. By
1900, despite heroic African resistance, that division had been
mainly completed. In that same year the first Pan-African Conference was held in London. Thus, at the very moment of the
completion of the division of Africa amongst the Western
European powers, the banner of the liberation and unity of
Africa was already raised. Today, of course, the question of the
unity of Africa is right to the fore of African discussion. The idea
first sponsored at the 1900 Pan-African Conference has spread
far and wide in Africa, taken deep root and become a powerful
force in African politics.

The fact that the first Pan-African Conference was held as a
consequence of the conquest and division of Africa amongst
the European powers provides a clue as to one of the main
reasons for the growth of this conception of a common destiny
for all Africans, of a common interest in their struggle. In short-
hand, one can say that the idea of African unity arose in response
to the forced disunity of Africa. The western powers had carved
up Africa; Africa had to be united to be able to fight back against
the oppressors. Moreover, Africa fell not into the hands of a
single power, as had been the fate of India or Indonesia, but into
the hands of a whole group of powers. To fight against this joint
strength of the imperialists required the united forces of the
African people.

An additional factor was that of racial discrimination. In a
memorial which Dr. Du Bois drafted for the first Pan-African
Conference appears the now historic slogan (which was later to

132

appear at the head of his influential book *The Souls of Black Folk*), "The problem of the Twentieth Century is the Color line". Racial discrimination has been practised in Africa on such a scale, and to such a degree, that the question of colour, of race, of a feeling by the people of Africa of their common destiny as victims of racial oppression, has become a powerful factor in developing the concept of all-African unity.

Elsewhere, treating of the problems of American Negroes, Du Bois has observed that common suffering rather than a common biology or ethnic identity has been the important factor in bringing them together. Thus, he talks of "a strong hereditary cultural unity born of slavery, of common suffering, prolonged proscription and curtailment of political and civil rights". What was true of the American Negro was equally true, if not more so, for the African exploited, tortured and humiliated on his native soil.

All these factors were present at the beginning of the century, at the time that the idea of all-African unity first took root. Sixty years of imperialist rule have only served to accentuate them still further. The division of Africa by imperialism was maintained, and even carried further, by the fresh divisions carried out after the defeat of Germany in 1918; and racial discrimination was intensified and institutionalised in the form of laws and regulations laid down by the colonial powers. The growth of migrant labour on a mass scale as a result of the destruction of traditional African agriculture, the introduction of hut and poll tax, and the imposition of forced labour and recruitment, have sent millions of Africans pouring across frontiers every year in their search for work. In the mines and on the plantations, workers from Nyasaland, Mozambique, Swaziland, Basutoland, Bechuanaland, the Rhodesias, Angola, Upper Volta, Nigeria, Tanganyika, Uganda, Ghana and other territories have been brought close together, suffered the same humiliation and exploitation, realised that they have the same common enemy, imperialism, and that their united effort is needed to win their independence.

The growth of national consciousness in the more than fifty-five differently administered African states and islands, especially since 1945, has stimulated political thinking and brought home even more to the African people how precarious could be the independence of a single African state standing in isolation from the rest of Africa. This is especially so in view of the coming together of the imperialist powers in N.A.T.O., one of whose aims is the defence of imperialist interests in Africa. On every side the African people face the joint front of imperialism, a front which still remains despite the very real differences which exist amongst the imperialist powers themselves. These latter may differ, for example, as to who amongst them should control the mineral wealth of Katanga, but they are as one in determining that, at all costs, it should not fall into the hands of its real owners, the Congolese people. The weapons and napalm bombs used by the Portuguese colonialists against the people of Angola come from N.A.T.O. sources, and are often "made in U.S.A.". Imperialist powers such as Britain and France hold up any United Nations action to take decisive measures against the racialist government of Verwoerd. American arms were used by France to keep down Algeria, while West German veterans fought in the ranks of the fascist "paras". Confronted with such a powerful alliance, the African people, the national organisations and the new states and their leaders are increasingly driven to the understanding that their utmost unity is needed to defeat the enemy. Collective colonialism and neo-colonialism must, in fact, be met by collective action on the part of the people of Africa themselves.

African Unity—a Progressive Conception

African unity, therefore, is basically a progressive trend, and is an expression of the desire of the African people to abolish the colonial system, end racial discrimination and liberate themselves from foreign rule. So powerful, in fact, has become this concept that no African leader can fail to give it cognisance, to express sympathy and support for it. Some leaders are more emphatic and enthusiastic than others. Some fight sincerely to strengthen this unity, while others pay it lip service. But there are none who dare to say openly: "We are against African unity!"

How important this concept has become was emphasised at the Second All-African Peoples Conference, at Tunis, 25–30 January 1960. Its Resolution on African Unity stressed that "the great conception of pan-Africanism constitutes a new element in the national awareness of the African people", that "the conception of unity . . . uplifts the African peoples" and that therefore it was necessary "to mobilise the African masses around this conception and to make of its achievements the fundamental objective of their actions and their deliberations".

Thus the idea of all-African unity has become a material force influencing all African national and anti-colonial movements, and shaping the policies and activities of the new states and their leaders. There are several forms in which this concept finds expression in the day-to-day politics and activities of the African people. First, in the coming together of the people's organisations. It is significant that Ghana, whose Convention People's Party under the leadership of Kwame Nkrumah has, from the very beginning, championed the unity of the people of Africa, followed the achievement of its independence in March 1957 with the calling, at Accra in December 1958, of the first All-African Peoples Conference. This conference was in the tradition of the previous Pan-African conferences called between 1900 and 1945—but now it was held on African soil, and in the capital of an independent African state. The All-African Peoples Conference has since become a permanent body, has held two further conferences, at Tunis in 1960 and Cairo in 1961, and has given considerable help to strengthening the united action of the African people, especially in the campaigns against apartheid in South Africa, in support of the people of Algeria and Angola, and in bringing solidarity to the struggle of the people of Kenya and the Central African Federation. In its wake has appeared the All-African Trade Union Federation, and steps have been taken to develop all-African youth and women's organisations. all-African organisations for farmers and for co-operatives are also being established. Other all-African organisations are also springing up, such as the all-African Journalists' Association.

At the states level, too, important steps have been taken towards unity. As early as April 1958 the first Conference of Independent African States was held at Accra. In its final Declaration it proclaimed *inter alia*:

"We resolve to preserve the unity of purpose and action in international affairs which we have forged among ourselves in this historic conference, and to safeguard our hard-won independence, sovereignty and territorial integrity and to preserve among ourselves fundamental unity of outlook on foreign policy. . . ."

The Declaration also contained a pledge that the independent African states would "co-ordinate" their economic plans "through a joint economic effort", embracing "co-ordinated industrial planning", an increase in trade between the African territories and the improvement of communications between them.

Since that time further steps have been taken to implement these policies. A measure of co-ordination between the African states has been achieved in the various bodies of the United Nations and at other international gatherings; and discussions have begun on various aspects of economic co-operation. What the people of Africa expect from their governments in the field of African unity is well demonstrated by the decisions of the All-African Peoples Conferences. At the first Conference, that of 1958, a call was made for the abolition or adjustment of artificial boundaries, the abolition of pass requirements and other travel restrictions, reciprocal rights of citizenship for Africans in each other's territories, the organisation of inter-territorial enterprises, the setting up of regional organisations of trade unions, political parties, youth and so on, and the amalgamation of independent states into regional groupings as a first step towards "a Commonwealth of Free African States". The second Conference, that at Tunis, in January 1960, called for "joint enterprises and inter-African companies", the "removal of customs barriers between the independent African States", the developing of economic relations "and the consequent setting up of an African Common Market", the formation of an African Transport Company (land, air and sea), the setting up of "an African Investment Bank to promote development projects", as well as the creation of "an African Institute for Research and Training of various cadres". In addition to such steps for economic co-operation, the second All-African Peoples Conference also went on record for the organisation of inter-African sports and cultural events, cultural exchanges of all kinds, the setting up of a Cultural Institute "in order to enable the African countries to benefit mutually from their respective cultures and to promote the development of African culture", the taking of steps to eliminate the difficulties caused by the diversity of languages on the African continent, and the founding of an all-African trade union federation.

By the time of the third Conference, that held at Cairo in March 1961, the experience of the African people had deepened their resolve and understanding that unity must be achieved. In its resolution on African Unity and Solidarity it recommended to all governments of independent African states that they create an African Consultative Assembly, a council of African states, a Commission of African experts "to elaborate a common economic policy", an African joint defence, and an All-African Cultural Commission. It further called for all-African organisations of trade unions, youth, women and farmers, and for the creation of an African Press Agency, an African Information Centre and a Free-African Radio Station. In the field of economic co-operation, the Conference called for the formation of an African Monetary Zone and reasserted most of the economic demands of the second Conference with a view to the establishment of an African Common Market.

Over and above these particular aspects of co-operation between the different African states and people's organisations is the conception of the political unity of Africa, expressed in the idea of a Union of African States. This idea has found a special advocate in Kwame Nkrumah and the people of Ghana. Nkrumah has repeatedly given voice to the idea that freedom and independence for Ghana has no meaning unless all Africa is free; and the Ghana constitution goes so far as to express the readiness of Ghana to surrender her own sovereignty if this were necessary for the establishment of a United States of Africa. Sekou Toure and the people of Guinea take a similar standpoint, and the preamble to the Constitution of the Republic of Guinea states that "Guinea unconditionally supports any policy aimed at establishing a Union of African States". In support of this idea of political union the presidents of Ghana, Guinea and Mali, three countries which had previously united in the Ghana-Guinea-Mali Union in December 1960, met in April 1961 and signed the Charter of the Union of African States, which they regard as the basis for the future Union of all African States.

Obstacles to Unity

Before dealing in more detail with this question of a political union in Africa, assessing what it signifies, and what difficulties lie in the path of its achievement, it is necessary to deal with the existing problems of disunity in Africa. As we have already noticed, an initial cause of the disunity of Africa has been the division of Africa amongst the major imperialist powers. Not only did these powers tear up the living body of Africa amongst themselves, but they did it in a manner which completely ignored the historic and ethnic boundaries which already existed.

As a consequence of the division of Africa after 1885, again after the defeat of imperial Germany in 1918, and yet again after the defeat of Italian fascism in 1945, there is a striking discrepancy all over Africa between state frontiers and natural ethnic divisions. Thus the Ewe people live partly in Ghana, partly in Togo, the Masai live in Kenya and Tanganyika, the Wolof in Senegal and Gambia, the Malinke in Guinea, Mali, the Ivory Coast, Liberia, Sierra Leone, Gambia. Kamerun, itself an artificial creation originally of German imperialism, was later divided between Britain and France, and though the two territories are now federated, they have yet to achieve complete reunification. The Somali Republic, itself a recent merger of former British-occupied and Italian-occupied Somalia, is still deprived, by French imperialism, of unification with French-held Somaliland; and there are also Somali people in Ethiopia and in north Kenya. There are two Congos, one former French, the other former Belgian, and Ba-Congo people also live across the frontier in north Angola. The boundary between Tanganyika and Nyasaland, too, is, from an ethnic standpoint, artificial.

It is one of the hopes of imperialism that it will be able to turn this situation to its advantage, to play off one African state against another, to cause divisions in the national movements, to tear off whole regions from independent African states, and to disrupt the unity of the African people. There is no doubt that French imperialism, when it transformed the former French Equatorial Africa and French West Africa into a dozen separate states, calculated it would be better able to maintain its influence throughout this vast region by dealing separately with a number of small states. There has been, too, no lack of endeavour on the part of British and French imperialism to play out their own inter-imperialist rivalries in Nigeria and the Cameroons, and in Ghana and Togo, as well as to try to score off the national movements in both cases by encouraging strife. In the same way, it was undoubtedly French imperialist influence which set Senegal against Soudan and so broke up the former Mali Union. Similarly, British imperialism has not given up hope of using the coastal strip in Kenya to aggravate relations with Zanzibar, and it is clear, too, that she is by no means disinterested in the possibility of strife between Kenya and Somalia, or between Somalia and Ethiopia arising from the existence of Somali people in Kenya and Ethiopia.

Of course, divide and rule has long been a weapon of imperialism, of British imperialism in particular. Thus Hindu was set against Moslem in India, Arab versus Jew in former Palestine, Catholic against Protestant in Ireland, Tamil versus Sinhalese in Ceylon, Turk against Greek in Cyprus. Africa has been no exception to this rule, though in this case refinements to the method have been added. Faced in the past decade with a growing insistence by the African people that they be allowed to rule themselves, British imperialism has worked hard to play on every division and backward-looking force. Its aim has been to make possible the creation of "federal" states in which feudal and tribal reaction would play a key role, and British imperialism would be left, in effect, to rule the roost from behind the scenes.

If anyone doubts this, let him read Kwame Nkrumah's autobiography and learn how Britain attempted this trick in Ghana. Despite the clear verdict of the 1954 General Election, which gave the Convention People's Party an overwhelming majority, Conservative politicians in alliance with reactionary chiefs in Ashanti, and taking advantage of the genuine feelings of pride and independence of the Ashanti people who had repeatedly battled against British imperialism in the nineteenth century, started a separatist agitation, hoping to secure a federal form of government which would enable them to resist and sabotage the central government's programme. This agitation was backed by most of the press in Britain, while the actions of the British Government, especially their deliberate failure to condemn the separatists, served, in Nkrumah's words, "as a stimulant to the unrest". By strong, decisive action, backed by the overwhelming majority of the Ghanaian people, the C.P.P. and its leadership were able to smash the separatist plot, and Ghana was thus enabled to embark on a programme of economic and social advance.

Though balked in Ghana, British imperialism scored a temporary success in Nigeria, making use of the feudal-led Northern People's Congress and of stirred-up conflict between the Ibo and Yoruba peoples, to establish a federal Nigeria and to ensure that leading positions in independent Nigeria would fall into the hands of feudal reaction.

In Northern Rhodesia, where the "threat" of independence draws ever nearer, the British Government has already made the first moves to foster a separatist agitation in Barotseland; and at the same time, across the frontier in the Congo, the same classic game has been played with Katanga, mainly due to British imperialist influence. In Uganda, too, it has long been the practice of British governments to play off the Buganda Kingdom against the remainder of the people, and even the latest constitutional proposals are designed to leave this division as a future source of friction and disunity.

Recent negotiations in Kenya, too, fully expose this tactic of ruling circles in Britain. In the 1961 elections, deliberately held prior to Jomo Kenyatta's release and his appointment as leader of the Kenya African National Union, that party received 550,000 votes against 150,000 votes for the Kenya African Democratic Union. Breaking a joint pledge which they had made with K.A.N.U. not to participate in any government of Kenya until Kenyatta's release, K.A.D.U., with the support of certain European settlers, including Michael Blundell's New Kenya Party, agreed to form a Council of Ministers, together with the Governor and his officials.

K.A.N.U., with support from all the different peoples of Kenya, stands for a united Kenya, for the formation of a strong central government which will be able to stand up to imperialism and plan the development of the country's economy. K.A.D.U., on the other hand, stands for a "regional form" of government which, if it came about, would allow full scope to tribal, parochial and separatist tendencies, lead to disunity and leave British imperialism in the background but with decisive influence and levers of control still in its hands.

Early in October 1961 K.A.D.U. put forward a detailed plan for a "regional government system" which proposed the establishment of at least five regional governments in a land of under 9 million people. (Later reports suggested that as many as eleven regions were suggested.) "The details of the plan", admitted *The Times*, "were worked out by K.A.D.U.'s European associates." Playing on the understandable anxieties of the Masai people, the Somalis, the coastal tribes and others, K.A.D.U. has stirred up hostility in the country and has openly threatened "civil war" if its plans are unheeded.

Jomo Kenyatta has rightly warned against the dangers involved in this agitation by K.A.D.U. "Regionalism", he has pointed out, "leads to a Congo situation, and we don't want that to happen in Kenya."

But the British Government evidently looks with favour on the proposals of K.A.D.U. In fact, on the very day of his arrival in Nairobi, during his visit to Kenya in November 1961, Mr. Reginald Maudling, Secretary of State for the Colonies, stated: "Clearly there could be a very great advantage in a federation." Later, during his stay in Kenya, Mr. Maudling explained in more detail what he had in mind. He spoke with approval of the idea of regional "governing authorities" with "their own defined rights" which do not derive from the central government. Significantly, he added that the powers of these regional governments "would be entrenched in such a way that they could not be swept aside as they had been in Ghana".

When, in the spring of 1962, the representatives of the Kenya parties sat down in London for negotiations with the British Government over the new constitution, British Government pressure and manœuvre, with the aid of the compromising K.A.D.U. leaders, was able to foist on Kenyatta and the K.A.N.U. leaders an agreement which went a considerable way towards introducing the principle of regionalism into the future Kenya constitution. There is no doubt that future troubles for Kenya are being prepared by these tactics of divide and rule which are being so obviously pursued by British imperialism.

Boundary Problems

No one would claim that the solution of the national question in Africa, the overcoming of boundary problems and the satisfying of the aspirations of the different peoples as regards their own traditions and culture, their languages and dialects, is an easy one. Sixty years of imperialist rule have played havoc. Nations are still in a process of formation. And the new states being set up do not necessarily conform with national aspirations or ethnic realities. If, in addition to all this, one takes into consideration the activities of the imperialists to exacerbate every potential conflict and difference between the African peoples, to weigh the new states down with a series of most acute problems in this sphere, one can readily appreciate how difficult is the task facing the African peoples, their organisations and political leaders.

In considering how to deal with this problem, the African people find that in addition to taking account of the reality of the ethnic and historical forms of association of the peoples they must also give due weight to their newer economic and administrative relations. Sixty years of imperialist rule and the division of Africa have created nearly three score separate administrative and, to some extent, economic units which today have a reality the same as that of historic ethnic divisions. The immediate revision of the political map and the scrapping of existing frontiers is not a realistic solution. Apart from the still existing rivalries in Africa between the imperialist powers, who would certainly strive to ensure that their "spheres of influence", including the new independent states, remained within their respective spheres, imperialist interests as a whole would not readily assist a solution of this problem in Africa, since its very existence is a constant opportunity for imperialism to sow strife and thus hold up the advance of the African peoples.

Moreover, some of the leaders and governments in the new states pursue policies which only aggravate the whole problem. In a number of newly independent African states the new rulers tend to regard their own personal and capitalist class interests as the main thing, and are therefore more concerned with main-

taining their own position as a privileged class, with the possibilities of growth as a bourgeoisie, than they are in the wider
interests of Africa as a whole. Parochialism is a common phenomenon in human society, and where it is linked with very definite
economic incentives it naturally flourishes. Africa is no exception to this rule; and moreover there is no doubt that one
of the calculations of imperialism, when compelled to make
political concessions and to hand over power to the new African
rulers, was that self-interest and personal enrichment would play
a part in determining the outlook and policy of these rulers.
That is why, even before full political independence was won,
imperialism took steps, through the payment of relatively high
salaries to members of Legislative Assemblies and to Ministers,
to provide for the African politician an economic self-interest
in the status quo. The £3 million palace built for Houphouet-
Boigny in Ivory Coast can be calculated to ensure that he would
prefer to remain "king of the castle" in his own home rather than
make adjustments to his frontier which would weaken his own
personal position and power.

Factors such as these make it difficult to find a quick solution
to solving the problem of boundaries and nationalities in the new
Africa. Moreover, even within the frontiers of the existing states
there are tendencies on the part of some governments to solve the
problems by a bourgeois nationalist method, and not by the
method of democratic consultation and recognition of mutual
interests. In essence the method of bourgeois nationalism is to
solve the problem of national minorities on the basis of the
principle of strength. The weakest goes to the wall, the interests
of the dominant group take precedence. In the long run such a
"solution" of forced unity is not even a source of strength to the
national bourgeoisie. A striking example of this was the experience of the relations between Egypt and Syria within the
United Arab Republic. There is no doubt that certain reactionary
imperialist influences were interested in seeing the break-up of
the U.A.R., but basically it was the attempt of the Egyptian
bourgeois rulers to dominate and exploit the Syrian people,
including even the Syrian bourgeoisie, which resulted in Syria's
reassertion of her own sovereignty. Thus the bourgeois method of
solving the national question, whether it takes the form of local
parochialism and narrow nationalism or whether it is expressed

in "great power" chauvinism and an attempt to dominate other peoples, does not help Africa to tackle this question.

Soviet Example

In the long run neither foreign imperialism nor the national bourgeoisie can solve this problem. Experience shows that only under conditions where there is no economic self-interest to be gained through the oppression of one nation or nationality by another can really harmonious relations between different peoples be established. The family of more than one hundred nations and nationalities living in the Soviet Union have established a form of relationship, based on mutual benefit and respect for all national rights, which has enabled rapid economic and social progress to be made even by the formerly most under-developed in terms of economic growth and social achievements. All the peoples of the Soviet Union have historically developed territorial borders, traditions and cultures. But they are all united by common interests and a common aim. For this reason even the question of borders loses its former significance. A few years ago it was found expedient to include in the Ukrainian Republic the Crimea, which had formerly belonged to the Russian Federation. The latter has a population of about 120 million, while the Ukraine has only about a third of that number. In area, the Russian Federation is more than forty times the size of the Ukraine. But the larger and more powerful was ready to give up territory and resources and, with the agreement of both Ukrainians and Russians, Crimea was transferred. In the same way Kazakhstan has voluntarily ceded the Bostandyk District to Uzbekistan, while Uzbekistan, in its turn, has transferred to Tajikistan large tracts of land adjoining this republic.

Furthermore, as between the different Soviet republics, mutual aid is constantly developing. For example, to exploit the Hungry Steppe, Kazakhstan, Uzbekistan and Tajikistan have set up a special inter-republican body. Similarly, there is extensive co-operation between the republics in the matter of gas and electricity supply. Azerbaijan supplies both Georgia and Armenia with natural gas. Estonia supplies power to Latvia and to Leningrad. A gas pipe-line is under construction that will supply the

Ural plants, in the Russian Federation, with gas from Uzbekistan. Uzbekistan and Kirghizia are assisting Tajikistan to build the 2·7 million kw Nurek hydro-electric station which will provide power for other republics apart from Tajikistan. Many other such examples could be given to illustrate the manner in which a division of labour has been developed in the Soviet Union which enables both the individual interests of each republic to be safeguarded and at the same time carry forward the general interests of the Union as a whole.

In Africa, however, the impress of imperialism still makes itself felt. Moreover, there are important differences between the existing states which make full co-operation difficult. Some are still under direct colonial rule. Others are nominally now independent, but still have foreign bases and troops on their soil, cadres of the former colonial power controlling the armed forces, and "advisers" supervising the ministries. A minority of the new states are sincerely striving to strengthen the unity of Africa and to establish relations of trust and mutual benefit between themselves and, if they are willing, with other African states. It is possible that, at this stage of Africa's development, one outcome might be the formation of multi-national states, established on a democratic basis and with full respect for the rights, traditions and interests of national minorities and ethnic units. Another possible step is the creation of regional federations, leading to a union of all African states.

Of course, the form of state structure or of federation even cannot be assessed in isolation from other factors. If one considers the question of federations of states, it is clear, from the example of the British-imposed Central African Federation, that a federation can be a bad thing, and can be used by imperialism to hold down the African people in the same way that it uses division and disunity. At the present time there has been much discussion on the possibility of the formation of an East African Federation, and, beyond this, even to a federation of most of east, central and southern Africa. The idea of an East African Federation has been a proposal of British imperialism for nearly forty years; and when first put forward it had the support of the white settlers. African opposition, however, helped to put an end to this move. Failing to achieve its East African Federation, Britain had to fall back on the East African High Commission, a body with its own legislative machinery and economic instruments, in many cases overriding the rights and powers of its components, Kenya, Uganda and Tanganyika.

In the last two years voices have been raised from among the African people themselves, advocating the establishment of an East African Federation. Even prior to this, the African national organisations in east and central Africa had come together through the establishment of P.A.F.M.E.C.A. (Pan-African Freedom Movement in East and Central Africa), so that it was perfectly natural that, as independence day neared, they should look forward to maintaining their close links with one another in the field of state relations. At one stage the idea was put forward by Julius Nyerere that such a Federation should be set up *before* the separate states in East Africa had won their political independence—and he even advocated that, to achieve such a federation, Tanganyika would be prepared to delay its own independence. This view won little support from the African national organisations in East Africa; and their viewpoint was adequately expressed by Oginga Odinga, Vice-President of K.A.N.U., when he declared that independence must come first, and that it was only as independent states that they could consider the forms of their association with one another.

There is no doubt that British imperialism still hopes to make use of the existing East African High Commission machinery, as well as of any future political and economic institutions which might be set up for an East African Federation, and there is a very real danger that such a federation could become an instrument of neo-colonialism. At the same time, a real grouping of independent, democratic states in East Africa, and even extending further afield, could make an important contribution to the anti-imperialist unity of the African people and could assist in the rapid building up of the economy of this region, in the development of full co-operation between the peoples, and the co-ordination of their political activities as well as of their economic plans and efforts. Uganda hydro-electric power, for example, could feed Kenya, and Uganda home-produced textiles could be expanded to serve all East Africa.

Together with the political union already achieved in West Africa between Ghana, Guinea and Mali, an East African Federation which was really expressive of the African people and their demands and was under their undivided control could make a valuable contribution towards the establishment of a United States of Africa.

Lessons of forming the United States of America

In discussions on this wider concept the example of the United States of America is sometimes cited. But if one is to do this, one must learn the lessons from America's experience. In the first place, the United States of America was only achieved as a result of the most intense struggle including the taking up of arms and the waging of a just revolutionary war against the British rulers. Secondly, after victory had been achieved and the new unifying Constitution adopted in 1789, the American people had to continue their struggle to maintain and strengthen their newly created unity in the face of internal disruption frequently egged on by the British ruling class who strove to take advantage of every fissure in the ranks of American unity so as to weaken the new state.

Britain's colonising policy in America had always been to keep the colonies detached economically and politically from each other. Consequently the thirteen different colonies tended to develop almost as small nations in the process of formation. As William Z. Foster pointed out: "It took the fierce pressure of the revolution to overcome this sectional development. Eventual unity was achieved only with the greatest difficulty, even under the life-and-death pressures of the Revolutionary War." (*Outline Political History of the Americas:* W. Z. Foster, 1951, p. 187.) Sectionalism was in fact strong enough to influence the Congress to deny Washington the necessary powers for a proper federal army and in consequence he had to rely on quotas which the Congress "advised" the respective states to provide. One authority has even argued that with a strong centralised army the war could have been won in six months instead of dragging on for eight years.

But even after the adoption of the unity Constitution of 1789, disruptive and separatist tendencies constantly manifested themselves. The newly won unity was threatened by the events following the Louisiana purchase in 1803, when attempts were made to form a secessionist Northern Confederacy based on Massachusetts; by the plan, backed by Britain, to set up a western confederacy based on the Mississippi Valley, 1804–7; by the secessionist threats connected with the Hartford Convention of 1814; and above all during the great Civil War of 1861–5, during which the British ruling class supported the slave-owning plantocracy of the South against the forces of the national democratic revolution.

A third lesson to be learnt from America's experience is that whilst European reaction, especially British, constantly strove and plotted to disrupt and hold back the United States, the most outstanding supporters of progress in Europe stood on the side of the struggle of the American people against foreign oppression and, later, against slavery and domestic reaction. Thus leading bourgeois revolutionaries—Lafayette, Kosciusko, Pulaski, Von Steuben, de Kalb and others—fought on the side of the American people in their war of independence, 1775–83; and the main weight of liberal and working-class opinion in England came down on the side of Lincoln and the North and against the slaveowners during the Civil War, the Lancashire textile workers in particular making great personal sacrifices through unemployment and yet resisting the attempt of the employers to swing them into a campaign to force Lincoln and the North to lift the cotton blockade. America's struggles for independence and unity were also highly appraised and supported by Marx and Engels, and during the American Civil War the International Workingmen's Association, headed by Karl Marx, conducted a great campaign throughout Europe to win support for the American Union and on behalf of Negro emancipation. In the ranks of Lincoln's army, too, many communists, such as Joseph Weydemeyer, August Willich, Robert Rosa and others held commissions and other responsible posts.

Thus, if the achievement of political union in America and the formation of the United States of America is to be taken as proof of the possibility of creating a similar union in Africa, then its lessons need to be remembered—that political union requires struggle, vigilance against the constant manœuvres of the enemy, and alliance with external forces of progress, including communists.

Political union in Africa, however, also involves further factors

which were not present at the time of the creation and growth of
the United States. The United States of America was formed
before the era of imperialism, before the era of great modern
monopoly firms; and in consequence, political power in the hands
of America enabled the rapid development of resources. Africa,
however, despite the winning of political independence over most
of the continent, still finds her economy, her banks, her trade, her
mineral wealth, even her land and agriculture, dominated by
imperialist companies, including those of the United States of
America which, through the growth of its own capitalist forces,
has been transformed from an historically progressive state in
the eighteenth and nineteenth centuries, fighting for independence
and democracy, into a reactionary state reaching out to dominate
other nations and to destroy democracy. Thus, for Africa, the
struggle for political union has to be accompanied by a continuous effort to drive the imperialist monopolies from the soil of
Africa. Unless imperialism is banished from Africa, unless every
political, economic and military root is removed, Africa's aim of
achieving unity will be constantly frustrated.

A United States of Africa?

It is sometimes argued that economic co-operation should come
before political union. Sometimes the reverse is advocated. It has
even been suggested that both of these questions are secondary in
importance to the question of immediate united action to drive
colonialism from its remaining stronghold in Africa. In reality,
all three go together. United action around current questions
and to assist the struggle in Angola, South Africa and so on,
strengthens the bonds of solidarity between the peoples of
Africa and thus facilitates both economic co-operation and
political unity. Similarly, the steps taken to develop economic
co-operation between the different independent African states
can strengthen their economies, help uphold their sovereignty
and thus put them in a stronger position to champion the cause
of those still held in colonial subjection. In addition, economic
co-operation requires the transformation of the economies of the
different territories which must inevitably weaken imperialism,
dig it out from its strongholds and so remove a major obstacle

to political unity. Further, experience in co-operation in economic matters makes the idea of political union more acceptable.
Above all, even if the achievement of political union is not an
immediate possibility, the launching of the conception, the very
idea of a United States of Africa, becomes a political slogan
which helps to mobilise the people, and to strengthen their
desire for unity by providing them with a perspective which can
arouse their spirits. And that is precisely why the Second All-
African Peoples Conference in 1960 emphasised that the conception of unity "uplifts the African peoples".

The aim of achieving a political union of independent African
states is a noble and progressive one; but it is important to understand the basis on which such a union could come about. Unity
between anti-imperialist states and those supporting imperialism
is not possible as a long-term proposition. Of course, even those
states which today lean on imperialism are likely tomorrow to
turn in the opposite direction. All these states are in a process of
transition, even those with, at present, the most reactionary
governments. The laws of this epoch know no exceptions. Life,
the logic of events, the pressure of the peoples, will carry such
African states further than their leaders may at present contem-
plate. And the existence of a powerful socialist world will assist
the peoples of Africa to create a united Africa.

What is likely to be the economic, political and social character
of a United States of Africa? There is really no likelihood, or
indeed possibility, that in this epoch, when the whole world is
turning in the direction of socialism and away from capitalism,
that a capitalist United States of Africa can be created.

Firstly, if Africa were to fail to expel imperialism from the
continent, a united imperialist agreement to establish, under
imperialist influence, a stable union of African states is not
possible, for it is inconceivable that the rivalries between the
various imperialist powers would not manifest themselves and
constantly upset any agreement reached between them. The
varying economic and political interests of American, British,
French and Belgian imperialism have, up to now, prevented
them being able to act unitedly towards even the Congo, let
alone towards Africa as a whole.

On the other hand, if imperialism is driven from Africa, as
assuredly it will be, this can only be achieved by the most strenuous

struggle by the African people and their organisations, a struggle in the course of which the democratic mobilisation of the people will be strengthened, the people's political understanding heightened and the leading role of the working class advanced. In such a struggle Africa will be able to rely on the support of the socialist camp and this, too, will influence the outcome.

Under such conditions, and with imperialism expelled, root and branch, from Africa, what kind of unity could be established? Would it be possible for fifty or more independent African states, each one under the rule of the national bourgeoisie, to sink their differences in the wider interests of Africa as a whole? This is hardly conceivable. For the national bourgeoisie the only way to unity is by domination, the weaker states being swallowed up by the larger. But the weakness of the African capitalist class in every African territory, and the stage reached by world society as a whole, precludes the possibility of the development of an African monopoly-capitalist class which could establish itself in one of the most economically developed or potentially richest territories and, on that basis, forcibly unite Africa. This would be unity based on domination—and such a union, even if formed (itself an impossible eventuality), would soon come apart as the United Arab Republic did.

Thus the very struggle to achieve a political union of African states will carry the African people forward in their anti-imperialist struggle, and open the way to a socialist Africa, the only sound basis on which a firm political union of African states could be created.

CHAPTER SEVEN

AFRICA AND THE WORLD

Sekou Toure once said: "Tomorrow the African states will come and sit at the councils of the nations and a new voice will be heard."

A similar thought was once voiced by Lenin:

". . . it should be perfectly clear that in the coming decisive battles of the world revolution, the movement of the majority of the population of the world, first aimed at national emancipation, will turn against capitalism and imperialism, and will, perhaps, play a much greater revolutionary role than we expect."

(*Collected Works:* Russ. ed., Vol 32, p. 458.)

Africa has for 500 years, and especially in the past sixty years, been used as a pawn by the western powers—but a highly valued pawn, a source of raw materials and a base for military purposes.

Africa's importance to the world needs little stressing. Her people may be poor—a natural consequence of colonialism—but Africa herself possesses vast riches, and potentially is far richer still. According to United Nations estimates, Africa produces 96 per cent of the world's diamonds, 69 per cent of its cobalt, 63 per cent of its gold, 48 per cent of its antimony, 34 per cent of its chromite, 37 per cent of its manganese, 32 per cent of its phosphate rock, 24 per cent of its copper, apart from uranium, nickel, coal and other minerals. Nigeria alone produces 85 per cent of the world's columbite. The Sahara's oil reserves are believed to equal those of the Arab peninsula, and her coal reserves to be 4,500 million tons. Africa's potential reserves of iron ore are estimated as at least 57,221 million metric tons, more than that of any other continent, and more per capita, too. Her water-power resources are calculated to be equal to 40 per cent of the world's potential. In addition Africa has 27 per cent of all the world's forests, and hence huge timber reserves; and she is a major producer of cocoa, sisal, palm oil, ground nuts, coffee, olive oil, tea, tobacco, cloves, pyrethrum and other agricultural products.

Now that Africa is gaining her independence she will, for the first time, be able to make a complete survey of her real wealth—and no one doubts that rich as Africa apparently is, she will, in fact, be proved to contain still greater reserves of wealth.

Militarily, too, in the eyes of imperialism, Africa has represented an important reserve. She has provided manpower in both world wars—though in neither case was she consulted. And throughout her territories military, naval and air bases have been installed by the western powers.

A Positive Gain to Progress

One can readily understand, therefore, what African independence means to imperialism. The very formation of independent African governments already means a threat to the remaining military and economic roots of imperialism in Africa; and complete liberation will mean their final end. Thus the independence of Africa will signify a great loss to imperialism. But the victories won by the African people in the past few years represent more than this, more than the taking away from imperialism of important economic and military reserves. They represent a positive gain to the forces of human progress. The votes, as it were, have been not merely taken away from one side, but added to the other. And it is this, above all, which is the really significant thing about the African revolution. The African people have strode magnificently on to the world stage. No longer content to be the extras, they are now insisting on being given a leading part.

Together with the independent states of Asia, the African states are playing a significant role in international affairs. In the United Nations, frequently in alliance with the socialist countries, the African states have spoken up for peace, for independence for the colonial people and against oppression. Outstanding African leaders are clear that their own struggle is part of the wider struggles of all humanity for peace and prosperity. Thus Kenneth Kaunda, President of the United National Independence Party of Northern Rhodesia, and Rashid Kawawa, Vice-President of the Tanganyika African National Union,[1] in a joint statement (Dar-es-Salaam, 22 February 1962), declared:

"The struggle for African freedom is not for Africa nor for ourselves alone. It is a part of humanity's struggle for a just and peaceful world. The active support and co-operation of the freedom-loving people everywhere is urgently needed if Africa is to move as quickly as she should towards true freedom."

Similarly, President Kwame Nkrumah has written: "The struggle against colonialism and imperialism is part of the struggle for world peace, because the liquidation of imperialism and colonialism means the positive removal of the fundamental cause of war."

Sekou Toure, too, has emphasised the world-wide nature of the struggle for peace and progress:

"The ending of imperialism will be accomplished by the united action of all the forces for peace and progress throughout the world, and universal progress will come about as a result of the joint action of all those forces which place themselves at the service of mankind."

(*Works:* Vol. VI, p. 379, August 1961.)

It is significant that the voice of the Afro-Asian nations at the United Nations has become so powerful that leading western

---

[1] Since then he has become Prime Minister of Tanganyika.

statesmen are beginning to express "alarm". As long as the western powers could wield decisive influence, at least when it came to counting votes in the General Assembly of the United Nations, they were happy to put more emphasis on the Assembly and less on the Security Council where the Soviet Union's determined stand against their war manœuvres and imperialist activities stuck like a bone in their throats. But the trick has recoiled on their heads, for almost with each passing month a new independent nation takes its seat in the Assembly and the weight of anti-colonial sentiment and pressure swings ever more steadily against western imperialism. Gone are the days when the American State Department could automatically count on twenty Latin-American votes; vanished is the time when the socialist states stood virtually alone in the battle for freedom and national liberation. Today, despite their hesitations on some questions, or the lack of unity amongst themselves, or even the tendency for most of the former French African states to follow their master, de Gaulle, the voice of Africa is increasingly being raised for peace and against war; and, in still more marked fashion, against racial discrimination and for the removal of the still remaining colonial regimes in Africa. Significantly the delegates from Liberia, a state formerly looked upon as simply a pawn in the hands of the American Firestone Company, today stand up in the United Nations and assail the racialists in the Republic of South Africa.

All this clearly shows that the African people, their new states, their organisations and national leaders, are determined that Africa's strength and struggles should not be confined to the goal of winning independence but that Africa should play a most active part in the councils of the world, commensurate with her numerical strength and political importance. In this respect, it is significant that the Third All-African Peoples Conference, held at Cairo, March 1961, adopted a resolution which demanded "a revision of the Charter of the United Nations, so as to give our Continent appropriate representation in the Security Council and other bodies of the United Nations", as well as in the General Secretariat. It is of more than passing interest to note here that nearly forty years earlier, Lenin, in the proposals he set out for the guidance of Georgi Chicherin, the Soviet Union's first People's Commissar for Foreign Affairs, who was then attending

the Genoa Conference in 1922, made the following point which
he numbered "One":

> "The novelty of our international scheme should consist in
> the demand that the Negro and other colonial peoples shall
> participate on an equal footing with the European nations in
> conferences and committees, and shall have the right to prevent
> interference in their internal affairs."

It was in line with its championing of the rights of the peoples of
Africa and Asia, a policy laid down from the first days of the
Soviet State, that in 1962 the Soviet Union insisted on and
secured the participation of several African and Asian states in
the eighteen-nation disarmament discussions which were held in
Geneva.

"Positive Neutrality"

No consideration of Africa's role in world affairs would be
complete without discussing the meaning and significance of
Africa's stand on "positive neutrality". On the eve of his country's
independence, in 1961, Julius Nyerere stated:

> "When Tanganyika assumes nationhood we feel that we
> will do so as a nation uncommitted in world power conflicts.
> We intend to remain without commitment to either side of
> the cold war. Yet it would be wrong, in one sense, to say that
> we shall be a neutralist nation. Neutrality is sometimes taken
> to connote an attitude of not caring. We do care very much
> about certain basic principles. We believe that our most im-
> portant contribution to world politics will lie in the effort to
> judge issues on their own merits and to take our stand accord-
> ingly."
>
> (*East Africa and Rhodesia:* 7 December 1961.)

President Nkrumah has explained "positive neutrality" in the
following terms:

> "The cardinal principle upon which the peace and security
> of this continent depends is the firm insistence that Africa is

not an extension of Europe or of any other continent. A corollary of this principle is the resolution that Africa is not going to become a cockpit of the Cold War, or a marshalling ground for attack on West or East, nor is it going to be an arena for fighting out the East-West conflict. . . . For the last ten years the tone of international politics has been set by the Cold War. We understand the fears on both sides that have led to this tragic polarisation, but Africans have no intention of becoming part of it. . . . I refuse to accept the dictum that if you are not for me you are against me. Our slogan is 'Positive Neutrality'. This is our contribution on international peace and world progress. It is in this context that military pacts and defence agreements between African states and former colonial powers and non-African nations are ultimately inimical to the interests of the continent as a whole. Since there is no suggestion that any African state has any aggressive intentions, such pacts and agreements can only draw the states concerned into the Cold War strategy of the bigger powers."

(*Voice of Africa:* October 1961.)

Both of the above extracts show quite unmistakably—as does, indeed, the whole record of the independent African states in the past two years—that Africa has no intention of "contracting out" of the world struggle for peace and progress. There have been attempts in the west to depict the policy of the African states in such a light, but the fact remains that as soon as these states commence, in the words of Julius Nyerere, "to judge issues on their own merits and to take our stand accordingly", that stand invariably, because of the very logic of the position, takes on an anti-colonial, anti-imperialist character that can bring scant satisfaction to western imperialism. This is particularly true of the most progressive African states, that is to say those known as the "Casablanca Group", who find that on such questions as the Algerian war, Angola, South Africa, or the Congo, it is imperialism, "the West", which is the enemy of Africa, not "the East"; it is N.A.T.O. arms which were used against the F.L.N. in Algeria or against the ill-armed Angolan patriots, while there are no Soviet, Czech or other socialist arms in the hands of Africa's enemies.

Or, once again judging "issues on their merits", take the

question of the All-African Trade Union Federation. When the genuinely independent African trade unions take steps to form their own continental organisation they find that it is "the West", in the form of the I.C.F.T.U. leaders, who strive to disrupt their efforts, not "the East".

Or judge economic policies "on their merits". It is the Common Market, that is "the West", which, in the words of Africa's leaders, threaten African economic development. George Kahama, a leader of T.A.N.U., has said "that if Tanganyika were tied to the Common Market, its people would remain forever hewers of wood and drawers of water for the industrialised West". (*National Guardian:* 18 September 1961.) Precisely the same point has been made by Kwame Nkrumah, who has stressed that the Common Market "is bound to retard the industrialisation, and therefore the prosperity and the general economic and cultural development" of the newly emergent countries of Africa, since it will mean "that those African states which were inveigled into joining this union will continue to serve as protected overseas markets for the manufactured goods of their industrialised partners, and the source of cheap raw materials". (Speech at the State Opening of the Ghana Parliament, Accra, 4 July 1961.)

But from "the East", by way of contrast, come whole factories and plants—as in Ghana, Egypt, Guinea, Mali, etc.—the wherewithal, in fact, for Africa to escape from being "hewers of wood and drawers of water for the industrialised West".

Or take the question of neo-colonialism. When the representatives of the African people's organisations, meeting in the third All-African Peoples Conference at Cairo in March 1961, came to consider the dangers to them arising from the development of neo-colonialism, they came to the conclusion that "such countries as the United States, Federal Germany, Israel, Britain, Belgium, Holland, South Africa and France are the main perpetrators of neo-colonialism". In other words, the neo-colonialist threat is a threat from "the West", not from "the East".

When it comes to the test, therefore, African states and leaders find that it is the western imperialist powers who are their main opponent, not the socialist camp. It is significant that President Bourguiba of Tunisia, who had so often in the past been hailed in London, Paris and Washington as "the great friend of

France" and "the most pro-Western African leader", was driven by the logic of events in July 1961 to order his troops into battle against French imperialist troops at Bizerta; and, in the course of that crisis, to appeal to the Soviet Union for help.[1]

The "Two Bloc" Theory

The aim of non-alignment and positive neutrality expresses the just aim of the newly independent states to refuse to be ensnared by the cold war policies of the imperialists or be drawn into imperialist military blocs and alliances. In fact, Nkrumah, in the quotation cited above, makes clear that what Africa is concerned about is the preservation of peace and of her own independence.

Positive neutrality, therefore, is an historically justified and progressive standpoint for those states engaged in removing themselves from the orbit of imperialism. It corresponds to the stage these states have reached, helps to weaken the positions of imperialism and makes a valuable contribution to the cause of anti-colonialism and world peace.

Spokesmen of the socialist states have, on more than one occasion, drawn attention to the valuable role of positive neutralism.

"Our stormy twentieth century has given a new meaning to the concept of neutrality. The following of a policy of neutrality by countries inhabited by a quarter of mankind,

[1] In the summer of 1961, after the fighting had broken out at Bizerta, it was reported that the Soviet Union had granted Tunisia credits totalling nearly £11 million for the purpose of building three dams and establishing a technical institute. This was announced by the Tunisian Foreign Minister who was then visiting the Soviet Union to seek assistance in connection with the crisis over Bizerta; a simultaneous mission, headed by the Tunisian Vice-Premier and Defence Minister, was despatched to the White House. The *Guardian* Correspondent (7 August 1961) reported: "Many Tunisians are smiling today as they read the banner headlines in the morning newspapers: 'Moscow will offer unconditional aid to Tunisia.' This, to the politically conscious town dweller, is the first firm and realistic offer of help this country has received." The same correspondent reported that the mission to the White House had proved useless. "The Vice-Premier made little secret of the fact that he had returned empty-handed."

under present conditions restricts the field of activity of the aggressive military blocs. . . . In effect, if formerly neutrality condemned a country to play a passive role in world affairs, today the situation has radically changed. The neutral countries play an active role by the very fact of their existence and by the example they provide."

(N. S. Khrushchov: Austria, 30 June 1960.)

Speaking to the people of Guinea (Conakry, 6 January 1962), A. Mikoyan emphasised:

"We value and appreciate very highly your foreign policy of positive neutrality. It helps to strengthen peace and friendship between peoples, it defends liberty and independence, it gives resolute assistance in combating colonialism and imperialism."

Yet there are those in the west—and some in Africa who echo their thoughts—who distort this just conception born of the African people's own experience into a "theory" of "two blocs", both to be regarded in the same light and treated in the same fashion.

Yes, there are two "blocs" or camps—or two "world powers". But one, "the West", is colonialist; the other, "the East", anti-colonialist. The west is imperialist, the east anti-imperialist. The west represents capitalism, the east socialism. The west is the power of monopoly-capital, the east is working-class power.

The defenders of western imperialism would like to disrupt the anti-imperialist unity of the African peoples, and, at the same time, keep them in isolation from the socialist countries—and they hope that the "two power blocs" theory will help them to that end. But who, after all, divided up Africa at the Treaty of Berlin in 1885, robbed the African people of their land, labour and resources, and has continued to exploit and suppress them for over sixty years? It was the west. Look at the map of Africa of twenty years ago. There was *Italian* Somaliland, *Belgian* Congo, *French* Equatorial Africa, *British* Cameroons, *Portuguese* Guinea and *Spanish* Morocco; and earlier than that, *German* East Africa. But no "Russian" anything. Against whom have the Algerian people been fighting for their independence, the west or the east? Against whom are the people of Angola now fighting, the west or the east? Who is denying liberty to the people of Northern and Southern Rhodesia, the west or the east? Who introduced and who props up the system of apartheid in South Africa, the west or the east?

Is it not a fact that the east supports the African proposal to make Africa a nuclear-free zone, while the west opposes this important contribution to peace?

At the United Nations it was the Soviet Union and the socialist states which initiated the debate in the General Assembly in September 1960 for the ending of colonialism—not the United States, Britain or France. The voting record of the major powers at the United Nations speaks volumes.

Time and again, when the question has been discussed of U.N. action to exert pressure on the South African Government so as to end apartheid, the western powers, including the United States, have either voted against or have abstained. Similarly, on the question of Angola, the strongest resolutions of condemnation of the Salazar regime's repressive acts have consistently failed to win any support from the western powers. In contrast, the Soviet Union and the other socialist members of the U.N. have always voted in favour of all anti-colonial resolutions and have often themselves taken the initiative on these matters. An analysis of the voting on the twenty-two questions relating to Africa and colonialism voted on at the 15th session, 1961, of the United Nations General Assembly, and covering such questions as South Africa, South West Africa, Portuguese colonies, Ruanda-Urundi, Congo, Algeria, as well as a number of issues of colonialism in general, showed consistent voting by the socialist powers in support of the strongest measures against colonialism, contrasted with consistent negative votes or abstentions by such powers as the United Kingdom and France, supported in most cases by the United States. More recently, when the subject of Southern Rhodesia was debated (February 1962) in the Trusteeship Committee, and again in June 1962, at the General Assembly, the line-up was again quite clear; on the one side the Afro-Asian nations together with the socialist states, and on the other side the western powers, with the United States' representative giving full backing to the British representative. The resolution sponsored by thirty-eight Asian and African nations was adopted by an overwhelming vote; and significantly, it was a socialist country, Bulgaria, which, with the support of the Asian and African states, secured the inclusion of the important phrase "on the basis of 'one man, one vote' ".

Or take the example of economic relations with Africa. The Soviet Union does not own a single acre of land in Africa, not a single mine or oil field, not one factory, farm or plantation. Neither the Soviet Union nor any other socialist country has a single rouble invested in Africa, nor do they take a single rouble out in profits. No African workers are exploited by Soviet employers or companies, and no African peasants have been driven off their lands by Russians. There are no Soviet "settlers" in any African territory.

But can one say the same about the west? Not at all. On the contrary, they own much of the best land in Africa, hold most of the mines in their hands, together with banks, insurance, transport, trade and industry. It is big western monopolies and groupings such as Union Minière, Tanganyika Concessions, De Beers, Anglo-American, British South Africa Company, Rhodesian Selection Trust, Shell, Pechiney, Lamco, Fria, Krupps, Thyssens, United Africa Company, the American Metal Company, Morgans, Rothschilds, U.S. Steel, Bethlehem Steel, Standard Oil, Socony, and so on, who have seized Africa's resources and who exploit her people. Millions of pounds are invested by the west in Africa, but still more millions are pumped out in profits.

Just to take one single example, the Nchanga Consolidated Copper Mines Ltd. announced operating profits of £20,694,522 for the year ending 31 March 1962. Profits of a similar order are made each year by many other major monopolies exploiting African resources.

N.A.T.O. and other western military bases are scattered throughout the African continent. There is talk of a new N.A.T.O. base in Southern Rhodesia. France is insisting on maintaining her naval base in Algeria. Fresh supplies of Portuguese troops have arrived in Angola and Mozambique. New moves are afoot to establish arms factories in South Africa with the aid of the big British monopoly I.C.I. Israeli arms sent to Western Germany have been used against the Angolans; and so have supplies of napalm made in the U.S.A.

But there is not a single Russian, Czech or Chinese soldier in the whole African continent; not a single Soviet military base or airfield. Nor is there a single instance in which the Soviet Union, or any other socialist state, has even suggested that an African state should provide such a base. Nkrumah's justified warning against Africa being involved in military agreements has meaning precisely because there are states which have military agreements with African states, there are states which have military bases on African soil, there are states whose warships cruise in African waters, there are states whose military aircraft land and take off from African airfields, there are states whose officers and privates are stationed in African territories. And in every case these states belong to the west, not the east. Thus Africa's just struggle to end all military entanglements with outside powers is—when it comes, in the words once again of Julius Nyerere, "to judge issues on their own merits"—a struggle against the western imperialists.

It is the western powers which formed N.A.T.O., C.E.N.T.O., and S.E.A.T.O.—in each case a military bloc dominated by western imperialism but involving, especially in the last two named, Asian states. Everyone knows that these same western powers have striven, for some time, to set up a further military bloc in North East Asia (N.E.A.T.O.), and that suggestions have been made to establish S.A.T.O. (South Atlantic Treaty Organisation) which would tie the southern half of Africa to a western-dominated military alliance. Everyone knows, too, that C.E.N.T.O. (especially during the period of the Baghdad Pact) was used to hold down the people of the Middle East; that S.E.A.T.O. has been used to support tyrants in Asia such as Diem in Southern Vietnam; and that N.A.T.O. arms have played a role in Algeria and Angola. It is these western military blocs which both try to ensnare independent states in Asia and Africa and which are used, too, to prevent the emergence of genuine independence where it has not yet been attained.

But what of "the East", the socialist camp? Has it not also a military alliance? Yes, it has the Warsaw Pact; but this alliance only came into being *after* the establishment of N.A.T.O. in order to meet its threats. Further, the Warsaw Treaty powers have repeatedly offered either a non-aggression pact between N.A.T.O. and the Warsaw powers, or the simultaneous dissolution of both military bodies and their replacement by a European Security Agreement.

But that is not all. The Warsaw alliance does not even include all the states in the socialist camp, confining itself only to Europe. Moreover, it never has, and does not now, propose that any other states, either in Europe or in Africa or Asia, should become members of the Warsaw Treaty alliance. It has not a single base outside of its own socialist countries in Europe, nor is a single soldier of any of the Warsaw powers to be found in any country except those who signed the Warsaw Treaty.

It would be idle, in view of the above, for anyone to argue that Africa is "equally" threatened by imperialism (the west) and socialism (the east). Those who try to argue this way are only repeating the arguments of the defenders of N.A.T.O., C.E.N.T.O. and S.E.A.T.O. who wish to confuse the anti-imperialist majority of the world and disrupt its ranks in the interests of imperialism.

Imperialism knows that it cannot easily fool the people of Africa into believing that it is their friend; but, nevertheless, if it can persuade them to isolate themselves from the powerful anti-imperialist support of the socialist world, it hopes, then, that it will be easier to control Africa. In this lies the real danger to Africa of the "two bloc" theory.

But the contrast between the two blocs is not limited to questions of military threats. Take the question of democracy. Who is it who, for decades, denied the people of Africa all democratic rights—the right to organise, the right to form trade unions and political parties, the right to take part in meetings, processions and assemblies, the right to publish their own national press, the right to vote? Western imperialism. Who today denies these things to much of Africa? Western imperialism. Who stands up in the United Nations alongside the African states and demands one man, one vote for the people of Central Africa? The socialist states.

Or take the question of national culture. Who stifled the ancient culture of the peoples of Africa, denied that they possessed a history of their own, curbed the use of African languages and imposed the use of foreign tongues in schools, law courts and other institutions? Western imperialism. Who crushed the efforts of the African people to establish their own independent schools in which they could teach their own history and achievements? Western imperialism. Who drowned in blood the efforts of the

African people to establish their own independent churches? Western imperialism.

The Cold War

Or take even the question of the cold war from which Africa rightly wishes to be free. Who is for the cold war and who is against? The cold war itself was an invention of the west. Even before Sir Winston Churchill gave it a new post-war impetus by his famous Fulton speech in 1946, its spirit dominated the history of Europe, and indeed the world. The cold war was launched by western imperialism in 1917, after the workers and peasants of Russia overthrew capitalism and took power into their own hands. The cold war is, in fact, simply an attempt by western imperialism to put socialism into quarantine, to prevent its "dangerous germs infecting" the workers in the rest of the world who might become so delirious that they would take it into their heads to imitate their Russian fellow-workers and over-throw capitalism in the rest of the world. The cold war is anti-socialism, anti-Sovietism—and its protagonists are the western powers.

In reply to the cold war the Soviet Union proposes peace, disarmament and peaceful co-existence. The west began the cold war, not the east. The west wants to continue the cold war, not the east. The east wants to end it and replace it by peaceful co-existence.

And yet there are those in the west—and they have echoes, unfortunately, in Africa—who so distort things that it is the Soviet Union which is depicted as the bringer of the cold war against whom Africa must be isolated at all costs. But isolating Africa from the socialist states is the very essence of the cold war. Closer relations between Africa and the socialist states, far from bringing the cold war into Africa, would serve notice on the cold war mongers to keep out and leave Africa in peace. It is those who cried loudest "Keep the cold war out of the Congo" that let imperialism in and handed over the people of Congo to the tender mercies of American and European imperialist powers. It is those who rebuffed Soviet assistance while clamour-ing "Keep the cold war out of the Congo" who betrayed Patrice

Lumumba to his murderers and Antoine Gizenga into the same hands. And all those who allowed themselves to be swept along behind the same misleading slogan cannot escape responsibility for the tragedy of the Congo.

Perhaps it is argued that the "two blocs" theory is a question of an ideological conflict between capitalism and socialism and that Africa does not wish to be involved in this conflict. But it is beyond the power of the "two blocs" theoreticians to prevent Africa choosing socialism. Whether Africa takes a socialist path or a capitalist one cannot be decided solely on the basis of someone's wishes—nor is it possible for Africa to find some "third" path, neither socialist nor capitalist, a new, hitherto undiscovered or even unimagined economic category and form of society. All societies develop according to certain basic laws. The African states which are now emerging are not fully developed capitalist states, but have only the rudiments of capitalist development. It is open to them to avoid taking the path of full capitalist development; instead they can pass to socialism without going through the capitalist mire. The African people themselves will decide which way they advance to socialism, whether it is through the longer and more painful route of capitalism first or whether they take the shorter and more direct road. And the choice made by the African people will be conditioned by the character of this epoch, an epoch in which the world is turning towards socialism and in which capitalism is declining. Already many African states have declared through their leaders in favour of socialism and against capitalism; and there is no doubt that tomorrow further African states will opt for the same path. In these conditions, it is absurd to expect that the theory of "two blocs", or the conception that countries travelling towards socialism should remain equidistant between socialism and capitalism, can have any lasting influence in Africa.

The western powers work night and day "to keep Africa with the West". Their phrase, not mine. When these powers talk about "keeping Africa with the West" what they have in mind is maintaining Africa within the orbit of western imperialism. One can search every paper and journal throughout the Soviet Union, study every speech by every Soviet minister, and not a single mention will be found of "winning Africa for the East"— for it is a cardinal principle of all socialist states that socialism cannot be exported. If Africans wish to learn from the socialist states they will be given every opportunity to do so. But no socialist state will attempt to impose its blessings on Africa against her will.

It is up to the African people to decide—and there is no doubt that they will do so. For that very reason they are becoming a little impatient, not to say suspicious, of those leaders who use the slogan "keep out the cold war" as a guise behind which they pursue their own pro-capitalist policy and pro-western orientation. It is, after all, no coincidence that this slogan finds great favour with the leaders of some of the former French colonies in which French economic, political and military advisers still play a dominant role.

Even those African states which display the greatest militancy in defending their own sovereignty and in combating colonialism sometimes disturb their friends by the sudden lack of resolution they show at the United Nations or in international affairs when questions concerning the fate of Africa are concerned. Thus it is that often it is not the African states, but the Soviet Union, which makes the principled stand on behalf of African interests, and the African states themselves which take a step backwards. Thus after the arrest of Gizenga, after the United Nations had called off its action against mercenaries in Katanga, and after the United States had clearly established a firm grip on leading circles of the Central Government in the Congo, it was the Soviet Union who urged a discussion in the U.N. Security Council—and the African states which displayed reluctance. Similarly, when the question of Ruanda-Urundi was discussed in February 1962 at the United Nations, it was the Soviet Union which urged the withdrawal of Belgian troops so that genuine independence could be enjoyed by Ruanda-Urundi—and a number of African states which were not prepared to vote for such a proposition.

Such voting at the United Nations has been ably explained by the Premier of Somalia, who pointed out that this is a carry-over of previous relations between the imperialist powers and the former colonies. Some leaders of African states have not yet fully shaken off their "fear" or "respect" for the imperialist powers; they still feel that they must depend on them to some extent, and for that reason do not wish to offend them. Consequently they take refuge behind the "two blocs" theory and refuse to identify themselves with Soviet proposals even though they know, in their hearts, that such proposals are in the fullest sense in the interests of the African people.

President Sukarno once said: "One cannot be neutral as between imperialism and colonialism." And neither is the Soviet Union, nor other socialist states. They are against imperialism and for national independence for all peoples.

Cuba, courageous, fighting Cuba, standing proud and free on Wall Street's doorstep, stands in bold and vivid contrast to tragic Congo. For Cuba, as Fidel Castro has explained, never fell for any theory of "two blocs".

"When the revolution came to power in Cuba, it had two roads; either to stop short, within the existing social regime, or to go forward; to stay within the capitalist system and the orbit of imperialism—within the political structure associated with Franco, Adenauer, Chiang Kai-shek, all the military dictatorships and French colonialism in Algeria—or to stand beside the exploited, oppressed and colonised peoples. One must bear in mind that there is no middle ground between capitalism and socialism. He who remains indifferent before the struggle of the Algerians is an accomplice of French imperialism. He who remains indifferent before Yankee intervention in Santo Domingo is an accomplice of it. The same for him who remains indifferent before Franco and the rearmament of German militarists, before what is going on in South Vietnam, the Congo and Angola. *There are some who think the Cuban revolution ought to have got money from both the Americans and the Russians—a sort of blackmail policy. But this base and cowardly policy would leave the great imperialist interests here untouched. Such small glory would not be worth the death of a single Cuban.*

This is the great dialectic truth before humanity: imperialism, and confronting imperialism, socialism."

(Fidel Castro: T.V.-radio talk, 1–2 December 1961.)

Because she recognises and lives by this "great dialectic truth" Cuba not only lives and breathes while martyred Congo writhes in agony beneath the heel of international imperialism, but Cuba marches forward with giant strides at a pace that no independent African state can yet match. Take the simple index of illiteracy. In one year of concerted socialist effort Cuba has abolished illiteracy—while in Africa it still drags heavily at the feet of progress.

When Egypt, in her moment of peril at the time of Suez, was in need of international support, it was the Soviet Union and the other socialist states which rallied to her aid and made the western imperialists think twice. When Guinea voted "No" to de Gaulle and chose independence, it was the socialist states, along with African states such as Ghana, which came to her aid, offered her loans and provided equipment and technicians to help make good the damage done by the French who, as they pulled out, took with them anything which would help Guinea's reconstruction.

Yes, there are two blocs—but what a world of difference between "the East" and "the West"! Africa will learn—in fact is learning—the lessons of its own history. One cannot treat "equally" an ally and an enemy. There is no "equality" between the one who robs you and the one who offers you help, between the aggressor and the one who comes to your aid.

One African leader, when asked what his people thought about the Soviet Union, replied smilingly: "Our people do not know much about the Soviet Union. For years they have been cut off from sources of information. But they say: 'The imperialists tell us that the Soviet Union is bad. So we think it must be good.'"

This profound wisdom of the African people will yet prevail over the activities of the imperialists who want to confuse and mislead African opinion. It will prevail, too, against those in their midst who, sometimes through honest misunderstanding but sometimes deliberately, repeat the western imperialist myths about the socialist world, and thus do imperialism's work.

When one considers that most independent African states have enjoyed their sovereign status for only two years or so, the outstanding thing is that already Africa is playing a key and active role in world politics. Her weight is increasingly being thrown on the side of progress and peace, and against imperialism and war. Despite all the efforts of the imperialists to drag Africa back into the mire of colonialism, to ensnare the African continent in a web of neo-colonialist intrigue and to continue to rob African resources for imperialist profit, Africa will continue to surge ahead, conscious that in a world marching towards socialism and away from capitalism, Africa, too, must make her choice and march towards the sun.

INDEX

Alexander, General, 53.

Algeria, African troops, 55; American arms used against people, 134; change of French policy, 49; industrialisation, 76.

All-African Peoples Conference, 9, 29, 39, 58, 64, 76, 77, 117–18, 134, 135, 136, 137, 150, 155, 158.

All-African Trade Union Federation, 123, 125, 135, 158.

Angola, M.P.L.A., 126; N.A.T.O. arms used against people, 134; U.N. condemns repression, 161; white settlers, 27.

Apithy, Sourou-Migan, 47.

Asia, land question, 28.

Azikiewe, Dr., 51, 114.

Bakary, Djibo, 92.

Balewa, Sir Abubakar, 51.

Banda, Dr. Hastings, 114.

Basutoland, P.A.C. influence, 126.

Bechuanaland, P.A.C. influence, 126.

Blundell, Michael, 140.

Bourgiba, President H., 158–9.

Bradley, Kenneth, 94.

Busia, Dr. Kofi, 109, 110.

Bustani, Emile, 17.

Castro, Fidel, 26, 168.

Central African Federation, British-owned press, 56; federation a bad thing, 145; individual land title, 29.

Chicherin, Georgi, 155.

Chilembwe, John, 34, 113, 119.

China, 43.

Churchill, Sir Winston, 165.

Cohen, Sir Andrew, 53, 54.

Communist Manifesto, 35.

Conference of Independent African States, 118, 135.

Congo, collective colonialism, 62; control of mineral wealth, 134; imperialist attempts to sow dissension, 140; Ten Year Plan, 73; U.N. action and U.S.S.R., 167.

Cuba, international policy, 168–9; U.S. base, 46.

Dahomey, relations with U.S.S.R., 47; revolt, 113.

de Gaulle, General Charles, 49, 50, 92.

Department of Technical Co-operation, 53, 54, 56.

Du Bois, Dr. W. E. B., 112, 126, 132, 133.